PALESTRINA

GIOVANNI PIERLUIGI DA

PALESTRINA

His Life and Times. By
ZOË KENDRICK PYNE

GREENWOOD PRESS, PUBLISHERS
WESTPORT, CONNECTICUT

Originally published in 1922
by Dodd Mead and Company, New York

First Greenwood Reprinting 1970

Library of Congress Catalogue Card Number 74-100831

SBN 8371-4002-1

Printed in the United States of America

TO

JULIA WILDE

PREFACE

WERE I to place on record here the names of all who have given me help in writing this book these few lines of preface would grow inordinately, but I cannot deny myself the pleasure of acknowledging that of the late Mrs. Edmond R. Wodehouse, in whose hands it would have been my dearest reward to place the finished work, and of Mr. J. A. Fuller Maitland, to whom my deep gratitude is due for valuable criticisms and suggestions.

For the translation of the Mantuan letters, etc., I have to thank Mr. J. M. Rigg, while Dr. Ludwig von Pastor and the late Dr. Bannister helped me greatly in procuring access to the Vatican and other libraries.

If the result of so many advantages helps any lover of sixteenth century *a cappella* music to a better understanding of the subject it will not have been in vain.

ZOË KENDRICK PYNE.

CONTENTS

With list of published works in chronological order [in brackets].

INTRODUCTION

CHAPTER I

CHAPTER II

CHAPTER III

CHAPTER IV

CHAPTER V

CHAPTER VI

CHAPTER VII

CHAPTER VIII

CHAPTER IX

CHAPTER X

CHAPTER XI

CHAPTER XII

CHAPTER XIII

CHAPTER XIV

LIST OF ILLUSTRATIONS

INTRODUCTION

IT is a characteristic attitude of the human
mind to suppose that what is removed
from the actual generation by some few
centuries is necessarily either primitive, childish,
or antiquated. To the student the fallacy of such
a point of view is at once apparent, and he dis-
covers that neglect and disuse are often the result
of changed ideals and customs. The unaccompanied polyphony of the sixteenth century is an
instance of this indifference to bygone things ;
a form of music so beautiful that it has never
been surpassed, but sufficiently ancient for its
construction to be generally misunderstood and
its evolution forgotten. Yet, intended for a
certain purpose, it has lost none of its old power ;
and this very noble and pure art contains a
regenerating force which was never more needed
than at the present time.

The explanation is a very simple one. Like
some stream, flowing age-long through its deep-
cut channel—to be diverted, later, by sluice or

weir, into a fresh course—so did music follow a certain line of inspiration for centuries ; until it was forced by fresh conceptions of progress to accept other ideals, aims, and developments. These, in their turn, acquired new rules of theory and practice, the old formulas were superseded and forgotten, the ancient boundaries of the art misunderstood, and the individuality and sensitive inspiration necessary to its interpretation lost.

That it is still capable of retaining its old empire on the modern world is shown by the terms in which Richard Wagner refers to a performance of Palestrina's *Stabat Mater* as " an absolute spiritual revelation which filled us with unspeakable emotion "—one, indeed, finding its ultimate expression in the Grail music of Parsifal. After that it is hardly necessary to quote his opinion that Italian opera is " no legitimate daughter of this wonderful mother ; " yet it was this new form of musical art which superseded the old. It was, indeed, inevitable it should be so, for the Renaissance fostered the growth of personality, an idea fundamentally opposed to the selflessness and objectivity of the old polyphony.

The following brief review of the causes resulting in the phenomenon of a *Giovanni Pierluigi da Palestrina* is intended as an aid to those who wish to understand something of the history and evolution of this ancient music.

It was Plato who said : " The movement of sounds so as to reach the soul for the education of it in virtue we know not how, we call music "— a definition there would be no difficulty whatever in illustrating with the mass in B minor of Johann Sebastian Bach or Beethoven's ninth symphony. To what extent the music of 500 B.C. fulfilled so lofty an ideal there is no means of knowing, but it was probably no mere coincidence that this conception of the moral value of music survived the fall of paganism and formed the strength of its appeal to the primitive church.* Be that as it may, these Greco-Roman melodies were adapted to sacred words and thus became incorporated in the ritual. They were handed on orally, for all means of writing music down were forgotten in the general decay of learning. In time singing-schools were established, the authority of which was so well recognized that monks were sent from far distant lands to learn the authentic melodies—either the ancient, or new ones constructed on these models—but some hundreds of years passed before this position was reached.

It was a foregone conclusion that the Church would breathe her spirit into song derived from

---

* This material has been exposed and classified by F. A. Gevaert in his *Melopée Antique,* and is there shown to have been derived from the melodies sung and played by Greek artists who enjoyed a similar vogue in the last years of Ancient Rome to that of Italian operatic artists in the early nineteenth century.

pagan sources, and the singularly beautiful product known as plain-song was the result. This early flower of Christian art was as the illumination of a missal, for it had no significance without the text it enriched and beautified. Until the sixth century it was the only form of music tolerated in connection with the liturgy, after which period hymns attributed to St. Ambrose, St. Hilary, Prudentius, and others were admitted. Written about the fourth century, these were constructed on classical poetic metres, which, converted into regulated musical accents, may be regarded as the ancestors of our own time-system. On the contrary, plain-song is not rhythmical but follows the inflexion of the voice in the ceremonial reading of the Sacred Text. Though now subject to a less strict observance of ancient modes it has retained its place in church use.

On the evidence of the oldest surviving melodies * the Greco-Roman theories were held authoritative for many centuries. The system of construction can be identified with the eight forms of the Greek octave scale, and even as late as the ninth century the theorists revert again and again to the writings of the Greek philosophers, even if these were often misunderstood for the lack of pedagogic example. But in the tenth century writers on music waxed bolder and advanced new

* Gevaert's *Melopée Antique.*

ideas, though the absence of musical notation seriously hampered their progress. Finally, it occurred to an enterprising musician that certain signs used to indicate accents in declaiming the scriptures might profitably be employed to show the upward or downward course of a melody. The signs to be converted to this use were termed neumes * and were "aids to memory"—a pictorial representation of the direction of sound by points and dashes first used in Byzantine liturgical books. Indication of actual pitch or duration was impossible, but the signs could, and did, enable a singer to recognize a melody, or to distinguish between two with similar openings ; and—this possibility once established—the development of a musical notation was clearly only a matter of time. Such, indeed, became imperative when the composers conceived the idea of using two melodies simultaneously. Even in this very primitive form of part-singing something more definite than a point or a dash was required to keep singers together. They quarrelled over the interpretation of the neumes, it took years to commit the signs to memory—in short, musical art could scarcely have made further progress had it not been for a famous monk, Guido d'Arezzo.†
Wearied by the labour of teaching his choir, he

* From *neuma*, a nod or wink.
† Now supposed to have been a native of France.

invented a system by which it was possible to learn to read at sight in a marvellously short time, and—as he quaintly put it—"clefs to unlock the secrets of the staves." It is not certain that he invented the principle of the stave itself. Before his time a line was drawn through middle C as a definite point and pitch from which other notes could be reckoned ; but he certainly carried the idea much further, and used other clefs for the range of higher or lower voices. Guido died in 1050. Thus it had taken several hundreds of years to systematize what every child knows to-day, for until this point was reached everything was tentative, experimental, and fleeting.

While theoretical principles were gradually built up, the early uncouth harmonies began to give place to other forms showing increasing resource and invention. For the first seven centuries the history of the Western development of music belongs to the South of Europe. Charlemagne's great love for and interest in the musical part of the Liturgy was the stimulus under which famous singing-schools spread over the rest of the continent, and now music tended to become international. First the Franks, then the English, after them the Netherlanders, bore the palm. Each influenced all, each carried the art a step further, each exhibited some national characteristic, differentiating its work

from that of other nations. The circumstance
of the Pope's residence at Avignon, at a time
in which music was ardently cultivated at the
University of Paris, had far-reaching results ;
for when the Papal Court returned to Rome it
was accompanied by the choir of northern
musicians which provided the Pontifical music
in exile. These singers became incorporated in
the Roman choir and brought with them the
New Discant.

Some reference has already been made to
the practice of putting two melodies together.
One still earlier was to double the melody at
a different pitch, with the result that a rude
form of harmony was obtained in consecutive
fourths and fifths. This so-called Organum now
ceased to please, and by slow degrees a new form
of composition was evolved, a union of two
independent melodies, at first joined arbitrarily
but gradually acquiring beauty and freedom.
Such was the New Discant which the Pope's
Avignon choir took with it to Rome.

It was a product born of many nationalities.
The French brought innovation and daring, the
English charm, expressiveness, and clarity of
sound, the Netherlanders subtlety and growth.
Taking into consideration the well-known conservatism of the Church, it must be considered
as a most important event in the history of music

that this infusion of new ideas preserved the continuity of the Roman influence and so paved the way for the florescence of the great Roman School.

The ascendancy of foreigners in the Pontifical Choir continued until the latter half of the sixteenth century. All the great names of the Netherlandish School are to be found in its annals, either as singers or composers, for the fame of this body of singers drew every ambitious musician. Music was on truly international ground in Rome, and the art of composition now began to go forward with what seems, in comparison to preceding centuries, astonishing rapidity. To dwell more here on the individual points of development is impossible, though a bare mention of the device of canonic imitation, destined later to yield so rich a harvest, must at least be made. As musical devices grew in number composers tended more and more towards intense complications. Especially did Flemish composers display so great and joyous an ingenuity in note-values and time-measurements that it is little short of marvellous singers with the necessary patience could be found to unravel them. But if the composers occasionally forgot that music is an art first and a science afterwards, they certainly put the finishing touches to the theoretical structure which the great masters of the sixteenth century were to turn to such glorious account.

There was, however, a forerunner whose work cannot be passed over in silence. This is the great Josquin des Près. The facts of his life cannot at present be ascertained with any certitude, but it is probable that he was in the Pontifical Choir during the reign of Innocent III.,* and that he was born in Hainault. He has been described as the first composer of genius, and he certainly conceived music as a living art, and not as a branch of mathematics. Dr. Burney devotes thirty-two pages of his celebrated history to Josquin, and sums him up as follows :—

" It will perhaps be thought that too much notice has been taken of this old composer and his works " (Burney writes about 1780), " but as he is the type of all Musical Excellence at the time at which he lived, the less need be said of his contemporaries, who, in general, appear to have been his imitators." At Josquin's hands music achieved a fully developed technique,† and was ready for the final development unaccompanied polyphony was to receive at the hands of Giovanni Pierluigi da Palestrina. Nevertheless this point had not been reached without much opposition

---

* Not under Sixtus IV. as previously supposed.

† For the student these devices may be rapidly enumerated as, I. A system of note-measurements. II. *Musica ficta* (the use of accidentals). III. Imitation and canon.

on the part of the Church. There was, indeed, an intermittent quarrel between the clergy and the musicians for a period of time running into centuries, from 1322 onwards — when Pope John XXII. denounced the fantastic compositions of the new school and complained that they obscured the sense of the sacred text. The musicians temporarily submitted, but towards the close of the fifteenth century the complaints were reiterated, and with reason, for the requirements of the Liturgy were overlooked in the triumph of the new technique, and the situation was aggravated by the vanity and incompetence of singers who exaggerated the new artistic devices. In the multiplication of voice-parts the sacred words were indistinguishable, and when the custom arose of employing secular melodies in the interweaving of the parts, the profane title of the song so employed was often that by which the mass was known, an obvious and just cause of offence to churchmen. At one time nothing less than the exclusion of music from the Church was in contemplation, but saner counsels prevailed, and indeed composers were not lacking who recognized the truth of the Church's indictment.

It was after one of these periodic outbursts that Pierluigi da Palestrina sprang to fame.* Any

---

* His full name was Giovanni Pierluigi Sante ; according to the custom of the times he was referred to by the name of his birthplace.

consideration of the life of this great man accentuates the fact that he was no meteoric appearance such as his zealous biographer Baini would have us believe, but the culminating point of musical inspiration in successive centuries. So much appears from the patient reconstruction of his life by later biographers who, put on the trace of such discoveries by Baini's monumental work,* unearthed documents and facts formerly regarded as lost beyond the possibility of finding. Although exception may be taken to some of Baini's conclusions, it is undoubtedly true that without his enthusiasm for the works of this great master it might have been impossible to distinguish truth from legend, by reason of the almost complete oblivion to which succeeding generations had consigned him. Even so, it is a common thing to find that those persons familiar with the biographies, for example, of Cimabue or Giotto have never heard of Palestrina, yet he was a contemporary of some of the best-known masters of the late Renaissance period, and was born in the first quarter of the sixteenth century. There can therefore be no reasonable excuse for classing him with the *illuminati* of a forgotten age, or for the assumption that his art, universally admired in that marvellous epoch, may be dismissed as either primitive or immature. The unaccompanied

* *Memorie storico-critiche sulla vita di Palestrina.*

polyphony of the sixteenth century is a finished
product, to the making of which went many
centuries of evolution ; a perfect means to the
end in view which, in St. Augustine's words, was
" prayer to God with song." The long connection of music with the Church bore fruit at
last and lifted prayer higher than human language
can soar; finding the right accents for pathos in
supplication, jubilation in praise, sanctity in contemplation. In other words, that consummate
mastery of the material was now obtained which
had already found similar expression in painting
and architecture. Of such was the great dome
to the new church of St. Peter : its aspect there
was power. Of such was the face of the Sistine
Madonna : its aspect there was love, Divine
Motherhood. The fulfilment of it in music was
no less wonderful, but just because sound is
transient, while the picture or building is (in
comparison) intransient, great music can never
make so final an appeal, or receive the same
instantaneous recognition. Nor is this all ;
music depends on a variety of outward circum-
sances before it can make any appeal at all,
so that it cannot undergo the final test of
property in the same degree as other arts,
nor command the same consideration from the
worldly-minded. So when, in the first decade
of the seventeenth century, a new personal and

dramatic element, with its attendant appanages of beauty of voice and form, *fioriture* and ornament, made its appearance, the old impersonal elusive art—in its very essence, opposed to all that is implied in platform or footlights—was superseded and the course of music was changed. It became more human, less divine. It exchanged its quality of ecstatic contemplation of the heavenly mysteries for one expressing earthly joys and sorrows. In other words, Mary, sitting at her Master's feet, was replaced by Martha troubled about many things. Men now took from the old unaccompanied polyphony its underlying theoretical structure, but transformed it for the development of recitative and fixed tonality, and though, for many years still, compositions on the old lines continued to make their appearance, they were in the nature of atavistic phenomena. The great Roman School was dead.

PALESTRINA

PALESTRINA

CHAPTER I

THOSE who have visited the picturesque town of Palestrina will agree that in no other place in Italy is the great past more vividly recalled to the imagination. Built on a spur of the Sabine Hills, Praeneste, its ancient name, was "a place of cool and fragrant breezes," and for that reason a favourite refuge of the Romans in summer. Livy laments that its pleasures seduced senators from their duties on the Capitol, and Horace and Virgil sojourned there. It charms even now in its squalor and decay, for though sacked and besieged on more than one occasion, it still retains magnificent remains of pediment, plinth, and cornice, nor can anything rob it of its lovely setting in the chains of Sabine and Alban Hills, or of the flower-scented breezes from the adjacent *campagna*.

From its position the town was considered almost impregnable. It was further defended by

fortifications, partly prehistoric, partly Latin,
against which the forces of Rienzi hurled themselves in vain. It had not always been so fortunate. In a quarrel between Pope Boniface VIII.
and its Colonna overlords Palestrina suffered
almost total destruction, and its adjacent acres
were strewn with salt so that no green thing
should grow therein. Rebuilt in 1447, the town
was again ravaged by Charles V.'s soldiery during
that terrible time, the Sack of Rome (1527), and
it may be that music ran an extreme danger, for,
according to the most reliable evidence,* Giovanni
Pierluigi Sante (generally known by the name of
his birthplace as Palestrina) was then a tender
infant. At a time when the high-born were
reduced to begging their bread, it is possible that
it was an advantage to be of mean estate ; be this
as it may, Providence shielded the Sante family,
although, once more, the town was almost
destroyed. Again Palestrina rose from its ashes,
and to-day it is not unreasonable to suppose that
the tortuous streets, picturesque town-gates and
fountains, the water-carriers with their graceful
copper-pots—even the shepherds in their long
wide cloaks and high-crowned hats—can have
changed little since this last upheaval, for they
are all survivals of a mediæval past.

Tradition identifies a rough two-storied

---

* The register of his birth has not been found.

structure as the home of the great musician's family. Built almost on the town wall, it is only separated from it at the back by a small garden. In front, an outside staircase leads to a *loggia* from which a once large room (now divided into four) with high open hearth is entered. Here the father, with his wife Maria Gismondi, lived, and here the boy Giovanni Pierluigi was born, probably towards the end of 1525.* There were two other sons, Silla and Bernardino, and a daughter, Palma. That their circumstances were not too narrow may be gathered from the fact that they possessed a house, vineyard, chestnut-grove, and other property, but beyond that, nothing is known of " Janetto's " childhood. It may be conjectured that he showed early signs of musical genius, and, for that reason, may have been placed in the choir of S. Agapito, there to acquire the knowledge of those liturgical melodies destined to shape his mind to its great end. But, whether climbing the steep streets to the over-hanging *Rocca*,† listening, as he went, to the *stornelli* sung by the peasants in the meadows below—those melodies of untold antiquity—or in the cathedral, following the hand-beat of the choir-master as he chanted the long alleluias on an Easter morning, it is certain that all musical

* Weinmann. See Chapter XIV. for evidences.
† The Colonna fortress.

sound was to him of deep significance, and that he was storing up impressions to be used hereafter for the greater good of his fellow-man.

Only twenty miles from Rome, Palestrina was thus near enough to permit of an occasional visit hither, and that the boy made the journey from time to time is certain. For the means of getting there, remained always the chance of a seat on horse-back behind a good-natured Colonna serving-man, or a place in the Bishop's train on his way to visit the Holy Father ; and the boy would surely make his way to one of the great basilicas to hear a mass by Josquin, or Dufay, or Pierre de la Rue. There may even have been members of the family residing in Rome, though the only reference to any is to be found in a document discovered in recent years, the will of the grandmother, Jacobella, widow of yet another Pierluigi, dated October 22, 1527, the very year of the Sack. From the character of the goods she bequeathed to her descendants * it has been surmised that she kept an inn in the outskirts of Rome.

But the year 1918 has brought to light other documents which permit a much discussed question to be answered—who was Pierluigi's master ? Tradition gave him a certain Gaudio

* In which are mentioned two daughters, two sons, and a daughter-in-law.

Mell, whom historians endeavoured to identify with the famous Huguenot musician, Goudimel, killed in the massacre of St. Bartholemew. It has, however, been proved that Goudimel was never in Rome. An ingenious attempt was then made to recognize Gaudio Mell in a certain Neapolitan musician, Cimello by name, whose pupils, in a dedicatory address, refer to him as learned in Flemish counterpoint,* but this, too, has to be relinquished by the discovery of what may be regarded as the truth. One legend,† for which any justification hitherto lacked, was to the effect that Janetto came often to Rome, and that, on one occasion, passing the great church of S. Maria Maggiore, singing as he went, he was heard by the choirmaster of that basilica, who, struck by the beauty of the childish voice as well as by the manner of singing, took possession of the prize for his choir. This story it is which receives some degree of confirmation from the facts recently discovered.‡ According to various entries in the Chapter archives of S. Maria Maggiore, it now appears that *Joannes de pelestrina* (sic) was among the six choir boys mentioned there on the date 1537, and that, in the charge of one of the chaplains, Giacomo Coppola,

* Michel Brenet in *La Vie de Palestrina*.
† Given by Baini.
‡ By Casimiri, and published in his *brochure* "Gio. Pier. da Palestrina." Nuovi documenti biografici Roma, 1918.

these were instructed in music by the choir-master. Further investigations revealed that Rubino filled that office until April 24, 1539, after which time the records are not clear. A certain *Roberto* is mentioned (of whom at present nothing is known), and not until December 6, 1540, does a name occur in the archives which may be taken as that of Pierluigi's master. This is Firmin le Bel, first referred to in the record as Chaplain of S. Bernardino and, on the 9th of the same month, as choirmaster.

If then Pierluigi was between eleven and twelve in 1537, he had over three years before him, after which his voice would no longer be available. It may therefore be taken that he was in the choir of S. Maria Maggiore until the end of the year 1541, the last year of his stay there coinciding with Firmin le Bel's first year of office. As is pointed out by the fortunate dis-coverer of these documents, the boy's best years of study were precisely those in which he came under the influence of the Frenchman.

But though these records are now silent, those of the town of Palestrina are not. An entry was found some years ago,* to the effect that, " towards this year (1540) one of our fellow-citizens, by name Giovanni Pierluigi, went to Rome to study music." The supposition is

* By Cicerchia.

fair that his townsmen had awakened to the fact that great things were to be expected of Giovanni Pierluigi—otherwise his absence would hardly have been considered a matter of public interest. The point, however, of importance here is, did Pierluigi continue his studies with Firmin le Bel ? There may still be an answer to that question, but at present there is none. Be this as it may, Firmin le Bel became *maestro di cappella* in *S Luigi de' Francesi*, climbing to the altitude of the Pontifical Choir on September 4, 1561.* In default then of absolute proof no more than a mere surmise is possible that during the absence referred to by the town archives the brilliant young fellow-citizen continued to study with Firmin le Bel.†

The next landmark in Pierluigi's life is fortunately less nebulous ; there is, indeed, no doubt about it at all. This is his nomination to the cathedral of S. Agapito in his native town as organist and choir-master. The contract was signed on October 23, 1544, and the duties were defined as choirmaster on all occasions, organist on festivals, and instructor of canons and boys. When this contract was first found there was

---

* Two compositions of his are to be found in Codex 38 of the Sixtine Chapel.

† Maestro Casimiri's comment is so amusing, no apology is required for quoting it here : "Oh, che forse i posteri ebbero a confondere un Mel ; e peggio ancora un Goudimel, o magari un Cimello, con Firmino le Bel? . . ."

some controversy whether it would not now be necessary to assume the date of Pierluigi's birth as having occurred some years earlier, for the appointment of so young a man to a post of so much responsibility was not in accordance with the custom of the times. Possibly the reason for this departure from precedence is to be found in the annals already referred to. If Pierluigi's genius was already recognized by the town, there would be no hesitation in making an exception to the usual rule for one so likely to confer lustre on his native place—a point of view which receives abundant justification to-day.

The next few years were probably amongst the happiest of Pierluigi's life. If he had not already reached up to Fame, no jealousies embittered his life ; if his income was small (his new appointment was remunerated at the rate of a canon's stipend), so were his wants, and he had no anxieties. Already a person of importance in his native town (he was not yet nineteen), he had ample time for further study, and was surrounded by relations and friends who would watch his career with affection and sympathy. Three years later he married the daughter of a well-to-do citizen Francesco de Goris, on June 12, 1547.

The personality of Lucretia, his wife, is never once thrown into strong relief, yet a tradition exists that the marriage was a very happy one.

The great musician was destined to live through much sorrow in later years, and it is good to know that in his home was one who would help him to find courage. It seems as if his wife's father must have died shortly afterwards, for Lucretia received her share of the inheritance in November of that year. It consisted of a house, tannery, vineyard, fields, and meadows ; with Lucretia's consent, Pierluigi sold the tannery in the following year.

For four more years the young choir-master continued to fulfil his duties in Palestrina, where grandiose ruins, lovely landscapes with Soracte and the Sabine Hills in the distance, and the vicinity of Rome must surely have stimulated his expanding genius, and, if he chose to mount the rock at the back of the town, the dome of St. Peter's, the goal of his ambitions, would beckon to him across the wide *campagna*.

Then a thing happened the significance of which can only be understood if we go back a few years in the history of the town.

On October 5, 1543, Palestrina received a new Bishop, in the person of Cardinal Giammaria Ciocchi del Monte, formerly Bishop of Pavia and Archbishop of Siponto. The son of a famous jurist, he was himself a man of great learning and artistic tastes. Obviously he had opportunities of observing the young musician on his visits to

his episcopal seat, and of noticing his remarkable
gifts.   He may even have extended to him his
kindly interest and patronage.

Great as his position was, it was destined to
become greater still, and in a very unexpected
manner.   The death of Paul III. on November 10,
1549, brought about an unforeseen situation in
the Papacy, for it occurred at a moment when the
dominant Imperial and Farnese parties were at
daggers drawn.   The consequence was that,
divided, they were too weak to carry the candidate
agreeable to their policy, with the result that
the weaker French party seized the favourable
opportunity to elect their own candidate, although
he had already been expressly vetoed by the
Emperor, Charles V.   This personage was no
other than Giammaria Ciocchi del Monte, who
ascended the Papal throne as Julius III. on
February 8, 1550.

Whether the ambitions of the young choirmaster were aroused by this brilliant event in the
history of the town, whether the late Bishop had
divined his remarkable gifts and felt that he was
worthy of great opportunities, for one or other
of these reasons the unusual step was taken of
annulling his life-appointment to the cathedral of
S. Agapito, and in September, 1551, he received
the office of Master of the Boys in the Julian
Choir, St. Peter's.

CHAPTER II

IF the preceding events be duly weighed it will be seen that it is not too much to presume an interest in the young Pierluigi on the part of Julius, especially if the Pope's personal idiosyncrasies be considered. Of simple, almost uncouth manners, most kindly disposition, his well-known love of music was only second to his passion for jurisprudence. Though we possess no information on the subject, it may be surmised that Pierluigi had given proof of capacity and zeal in teaching the choir of S. Agapito, while his personality and genius marked him out for higher opportunities still. He had been trained at one of the most important centres of church-music in Rome, and in all probability the Pope saw in him a fit instrument for work he had very much at heart. This was the reconstruction of the Julian Choir, a foundation created by his predecessor, Julius II., and intended to fulfil a certain purpose dear to the hearts of the Romans, no other than the attempt to remedy the state of things brought about by the infusion of foreigners into the

Pontifical or Sixtine Choir in 1377, and who remained paramount there ever since.

It is not difficult to understand that the preponderating number of Flemish, French, and Spanish musicians in the Pope's service hit the notoriously jealous Romans in a very tender place, namely, their vanity, and they made humble protests. Julius II. admitted their legitimate ground for discontent, and partly in order to remove it, partly to create a convenient training-school, founded the Julian Choir. This supplied the services of the Basilica, and, at the same time, trained boys in the traditions of the Pontifical Choir, which celebrated body did not necessarily sing in the offices of St. Peter, but was attached to the Papal Court for the immediate service of the Pontiff, being in attendance at all religious functions and ceremonies at which the Holy Father himself was present, and accompanying him on his State journeys through his dominions. It was, in short, as much an adjunct of the Pontifical pomp as the Papal Chamberlains, or the Gentlemen of the Guard.

In the creation of the Julian Choir nothing drastic was undertaken. Its effect was intended to be entirely gradual. By 1526 there was a list of sixteen singers on its books, and its charter was consolidated by Paul III. ; in 1534 a gymnasium or school was attached in accordance with the will of Julius II., who left funds for masters *in musica et cantû et in grammatica.* A year later, the proportion of native singers in the Pontifical Choir had risen to seven in twenty-two. Not before the close of the century, however, was its purpose fully effected, when no foreigners remained in the Pontifical Choir.

It seems probable then that it was the Pope's personal wish that the choir-master of his former cathedral should be offered the post of *magister in musica et cantû* in an institution to which he attached so great an importance. The first notice to that effect in the archives of the *Cappella Giulia* is dated November, 1551, Pierluigi is referred to as *Magister Joannes*, and three boys are assigned to his charge.

The change from the little country-town to the capital of the world with its brilliant life of the late Renaissance was as twilight to sunlight. The lustre of the present period is too well known to need insistence here, but it may be recalled that the works of Raphael, Michelangelo, Cellini, with a host of lesser names, in all their fresh colours, marbles, and metals, adorned the churches and palaces; that, everywhere, wonderful new buildings, in sharp contrast to the narrow filthy streets of mediæval Rome; such piles as the Farnese and Farnesina palaces; the new wide access to the Capitoline Hill with its flanking

palaces designed by Michelangelo; the Via Giulia,
due to the wealth of the Florentine magnates;
and—most wonderful of all—the great mass of
new St. Peter's, rising foot by foot to the south
and west of the old basilica ;—all created an atmosphere of power, growth, and beauty that could
not but quicken and mature Pierluigi's genius.
Times were changed, indeed, from those in which
the little Janetto trembled at the master's frown
in the choir-school of S. Maria Maggiore ; when
he, with others clustered round a great volume,
must school his young shrill voice to the appointed
entry in a difficult piece of counterpoint, or to the
requisite length of a pause.   Now he had become
part and parcel of the great religious organization
to which St. Peter's was head and front, must
sign his goings and comings in its book, must
take his share in responsibilities connected with
its service.   Anxiety, too, as well as pride, would
be in his heart, for he must justify his appointment before a hundred jealous observers, and
hold his own in an artistic world governed by
foreigners of the greatest reputation.

In the eclectic group concentrated around the
Papal throne all the elements existed helpful to
the arts.   Not, indeed, a Mæcenas such as Leo X.,
Julius possessed a social habit of mind and extended his patronage not only to music for ecclesiastical purposes, but to that intended for festive

occasions from which he saw no reason to abstain.
In the chronicle of his reign there is frequent
reference to the Pope's presence at plays and
banquets in which music is either mentioned or
inferred, and it may very well be that the young
magister's duties did not end with the church-
functions or in the choir-school, and that his
choristers' voices were occasionally employed in
singing the famous madrigals of Arcadelt and
Willaert before the Pope's guests. The merry
or sentimental words would constitute no barrier
to their performance before a Humanist Pope
such as Julius III. was by education and inclination, who perceived no incongruity in assisting at
the representation of a play by Plautus, or in
patronizing an Aretino. Such influences were
certainly valuable in ripening and mellowing Pierluigi's genius, trained, as it undoubtedly was, in
all the erudition and crudities of the Netherlands
school.

But the sun was setting on Rome of the
Renaissance, with its social and political life
in contradiction with the ideals of a pure Church.
A growing spirit of discontent had already found
expression in the long fight over the recent
Papal elections,* and in every branch of society
these ideas were steadily gaining ground. The

---

* It may be of interest to recall that the saintly Englishman,
Cardinal Pole, was at one moment a prominent candidate for the
Papacy because of his well-known and burning zeal for reform.

discussions in the Council of Trent were the outward and visible signs of the doubt and distrust excited in men's minds by the prevailing laxity and irreligion. The need for reform was felt everywhere, even in music. The religious spirit did not here find adequate expression, and the requirements of the ritual were too lightly considered. The first breath of the new spirit was already to be found in the compositions of Costanzo Festa, whose death is recorded in the archives of the Pontifical Choir on the date April 10, 1545. His work shows some perception of the Josquinian theory that the sentiment was important and that a necessity existed of fitting the composition to the character of the words. Quite as remarkable was his recognition of the principle that the intelligibility of the words must not be lost in the weaving of the parts. It was a notable step in advance when music was seen to be far more than a mere embellishment to the ritual ; to be nothing less than a form, and a very beautiful one, of prayer if conceived in that high spirit—a conception lost sight of when the ancient melodies gave place to the subtleties of a developing technique.

But there was yet another element in Roman music at this period. In the Pontifical Choir were many Spaniards in whose compositions an austere, idealistic tendency was to be found.

Morales, a contemporary of Festa's, was undoubtedly the greatest of these. A sentence of this grave, ascetic musician curiously recalls the old pagan philosopher's definition.* " Music," Morales asserted, " should be to educate the soul in strength and nobility," and here is the measure of the man's art.

Thus Pierluigi arrived in Rome at the psychological moment. The old ideals were changing, and dexterity and scholarship had revealed themselves as insufficient. But as yet there was no master-spirit to fuse the different eleme ts into a perfect whole. Fresh to all these influences, Pierluigi showed later that he had been quick to grasp their significance. He was, of course, thoroughly acquainted with the two noble volumes of Morales's works, though the Spaniard had already quitted Rome before the younger master's arrival.

For three years the records of Pierluigi's Roman life are silent. It was certainly fully occupied. On the list of the Julian Choir were now sixteen singers, and the training of such a choir was no sinecure, involving infinitely more labour than that required in teaching the modern chorister. It may interest those unacquainted with the technique of the ancient music to learn what some of these difficulties were.

* See Introduction, p. xv.

C

Contrapuntal music was essentially a structure made up of many melodies. One of these, termed the *cantus firmus*, or firm-song, was assigned the chief place, and formed the frame around which the others were adjusted. While obeying strict laws in relation to the *cantus firmus*, within the limit of those laws the accompanying melodies may be said to have enjoyed equality, no voice taking precedence of another ; a fundamental contrast to the modern harmonic system with its indispensable bass and treble. In illustration of this point some directions given by Pierluigi, on presenting a copy of a mass to the choir of *S. Maria Maggiore*, may be quoted here. He says that if it is not convenient to have the top-voice part sung this is of no consequence, the composition will still sound beautiful ! Thus, each singer had necessarily to be self-dependent as there was no leader who might be relied upon at the beginning and ending of a melody, nor did the duration coincide. This was not the worst of it. The time-system of the day was a very pit for the unwary. A device at the beginning served to indicate the value of the division of the longest note, but even so, this varied according to *position*. As there were few bars, there were no strong and weak beats succeeding each other automatically at predetermined intervals, no definite pulsations according to a time-signature ;

thus the singer must give close attention and
possess an accurate knowledge of the elaborate
system of time-values. The modern musician
would regard the disadvantages of such a method
as almost insuperable, but there were great com-
pensations ; an exquisite quality of smoothness,
freedom from a foregone conclusion, and suggestion of soaring infinity, the ear never becoming
satiated. Other difficulties with which the un-
happy singer must contend included the necessity
of translating canon at sight (*i.e.* of repeating a
melody at the fourth, fifth, octave, or whatever
the interval selected) according to strict but un-
written laws, being forced to fill up the part
from his theoretical knowledge ; he must learn,
also, the compound divisions of time-measurements, so complicated that the most learned
professor to-day might well hesitate before such
a task. All this required unremitting labour on
the master's part and a corresponding expenditure
of time, for without accuracy and certainty, no
singer could hope to hold his own in the single-
stave parts which were all he had to sing from.
In spite, however, of the work implied in
training his sixteen singers, Pierluigi must have
been deeply engaged in composition, though in
this connection nothing appears before 1554 when
his madrigal, " *Con dolce altiero*," was published
by Gardano of Venice in a collection described

on the title-page as *Il quarto libro de Madrigali a quattro voci a note bianche.* There was nothing unusual in this, for church musicians had long ceased to regard secular music as derogatory, and Costanzo Festa, with Willaert, the celebrated choir-master of St. Mark's in Venice, were excuse enough were any needed. Times were to change again, later on, and Pierluigi would think it necessary to express regret for his madrigals as follies of youth, but while Julius III. was on the Papal throne, he was sure of encouragement and praise. Indeed, it may be conjectured that this first fruit of his protégé's pen did not escape being sung in the presence of the Pontiff.

But, this same year, Pierluigi brought out a far more convincing proof of his quality, both as scholar and musician. This was the first book of masses, described by a modern historian as the most notable dedication which fell to the lot of Julius, for, as was only to be expected, Pierluigi inscribed them to his great patron.*

On the first page appears :—

Joannis Petri|Loisij|Praenestini|in basilica|St. Petri de urbe capellae Magistri Missarum Liber Primus

with the publishers' names: *Valerio et Aloysio Dorico* 1554. Four of the masses were for four voices, one for five. The dedication runs as follows :—

* Von Pastor, *Geschichte der Päpste,*

Julio Tertio. Pont. Max.

Jo. Petrus Loysius Praenestinus

*Christianas summi Dei laudes exquisitioribus
rithmis cum cecinissem paucis ante diebus ; nulli magis
quam tuo nomini eas dicare visum est ; non eo solum
nomine quod tu unus in terris proxime ad Deum
accedis ; sed quod natura ita Musicae faves ; ut
sperare mihi posse videar, non ingratum futurum si
tuae Sanctitatis dignas aeterno praeconio laudes post
Deum cantare aggrediar ; quod mihi diu facere ut
contingat, non minus peto quam opto.   Vale.*

Which rendered freely into English is :—

"A few days ago, having set to music in a more
exquisite manner these Christian praises to the
most high God, no other name but yours seemed
worthy of the dedication, not only because you
alone are next to God on earth, but because you
are so disposed by nature to encourage music, that
I may hope that it will not be unacceptable to you
if I sing your praise after that of God and that I
may well be permitted this favour for a long time
is both my wish and my prayer.   Farewell."

A quaint woodcut represents Pierluigi on his
knees, offering a copy of his work to the Pontiff.
Both the portraits are disappointing, for though it
is well known that Julius' appearance was bluff
and almost jovial, the features blunt and coarsely
cut, these characteristics are here exaggerated and
give no hint of the real culture behind.   The
musician's face is equally uncharacteristic ; it is

indeed almost boorish, and without a trace of sensibility. But, if the portraits must be regarded as entirely inadequate, the dedication, at least, serves to give us a glimpse into Pierluigi's mind concerning his own work. "A more exquisite manner," he says, with pardonable pride. The technique is already there if the mastery which in a few years more would astonish the world is not yet full-blown. The tone is striking if it be considered that the words are those of a young composer offering his first important work to the head of Christendom. It indicates the power and conviction of genius.

If the adulatory tone of the dedication offends, it should be remembered that thus was the custom of the times, and that such phrases were as the Court-suit of a subject about to enter the presence of his Sovereign.

Of Julius' reception of the momentous volume there is no record, but when we read that the striking of a fine medal in this reign was celebrated *hilaritate publica*—with public joy—it can hardly be doubted that Pierluigi's masses were duly fêted. He was, moreover, soon to receive a signal proof of the Pope's favour ; but of that later.

On opening the book the fact is at once patent that Pierluigi was steeped in the learning of the Netherlanders. The first mass, *Ecce Sacerdos*

Magnus contains examples of Mode, Time, and
Prolation (as the different divisions of note-
values were termed) which the school of Josquin
itself might have envied, as well as instances of
augmentation, and combinations of duple and
triple rhythms such as only a close student of
these matters can hope to elucidate. But the
most curious feature of the whole, one which is
not to be recognized without a smile, is the
delicate compliment implied, not only in the title
of the mass, but in the treatment of the theme to
which the words are fitted. Pierluigi has at one
and the same time seized the opportunity of
praising the Church and the Pope, his patron, in
such a masterly compound of learning and
diplomacy that one hardly knows which to admire
most, the courtier or the scholar. Through every
voice-part, throughout each division of the mass,
stalking through Kyrie, Credo, and Sanctus,
Ecce Sacerdos Magnus continues its uninterrupted
progress to a melody which suggests nothing so
much as a folksong rung out on a carillon against
the delicate tracery of a Gothic spire in Flanders.
Could some fifteenth-century Fleming be re-
embodied, on hearing this, he would surely
stretch his arms and roll out the words with zest.
But *not* if he heard the melody wound in the fibre
of the mass itself. It would be as easy to find
the proverbial needle in the haystack. For it may

be compared to the warp on which the web is woven. It *was* the warp, the *cantus firmus* the " firm song " on which the changing melodies broke and receded like the waves over a hidden rock on the shore. This curious custom of employing an obviously secular melody in a composition for church use will be referred to at greater length, but, for the present, we will pass on, merely pausing to give the fine old melody as it stands.

It seems almost superfluous to point out that the homage before St. Peter's successor was a great deal more than an adroit flattery. There was inevitably a fastidious joy in the delicacy of the workmanship, in the envelope which contained the compliment. There is a suggestion here of the naïve self-congratulation displayed by Pierluigi's great contemporary, Benvenuto Cellini, on the completion of some object of beauty, conceived by his genius.

The other masses contained in this volume were *O Regem Cœli, Virtute Magna, Gabriel Arcangelus*—these for four voices—and *Ad Cœnam agni providi* for five. In all of these Pierluigi employs the same learned style and complication of device, but in *Virtute Magna* there are intricacies of complex proportion, *i.e.* subdivisions of time according to a duple and triple rhythm, which make it extremely probable that it would have remained sealed in recent times to all but the antiquary were it not for the elucidation given by the indefatigable editor, Dr. Haberl, of the collected edition of Pierluigi's works, who translated it into modern time-measurement. In spite, however, of the tremendous subtleties, there is a lightness of treatment, a freedom of melodic phrase such as no mere dry-as-dust pedant steeped in the accumulated learning of centuries would have achieved. If Pierluigi set himself the task of disarming criticism by a display of erudition calculated to dazzle his critics, he certainly succeeded ; simultaneously gathering up his strength for a fresh advance.

As far as is known, the Pontifical Choir, notoriously jealous of musicians outside its ranks, especially when of native origin, took no notice of these masses ; that they were performed by the Julian Choir was not only a foregone conclusion, but seems clear from an entry in its archives. There it is set forth that, in November, 1554, a payment was made to one Giovanni Belardino (*sic*) Pierluigi for the purchase of a first book of masses : this Giovanni Belardino was presumably

Pierluigi's brother Bernardino who, in that case, must have followed his great brother to Rome.*

One of the results involved in the publication of these masses was certainly the wider recognition of the young composer's genius. He was now a marked man in the world of artists and *cognoscenti*, yet he did not for that reason neglect the daily routine of his work in St. Peter's, to which what may be regarded as indirect allusion is made in the account given by a travelling German of his visit to the Eternal City about this time in Holy Week, when he speaks of the great beauty of the services both in St. Peter and St. John Lateran. If only he had been more precise in his commendations and had informed us what were the masses he heard!

* See page 39, footnote.

CHAPTER III

IN January, 1555, Pierluigi became a member of the Pontifical Choir. The mandate was in the Pope's own handwriting. Thus, in the short space of four years, he reached a position coveted by the most renowned musicians of Europe.

The entry in the Choir records, made by the *Puntatore*, or registrar, is as follows :—

"Dominica 13 Jan fuit ad missus (*sic*) in nobum (*sic*) cantorem Joannes de palestrina de mandatu (*sic*) S mi D. Julii absque ulo (*sic*) examine et secundum motum proprium quod habebamus et absque consensu cantorum ingresus (*sic*) fuit." *

That is to say, Pierluigi was admitted in accordance with the will of his all-powerful protector, without being subjected to an entrance examination ; moreover, the singers themselves had not voted in favour of his election. Though, on the face of it, it would seem that Pierluigi's claims were of the highest order, this autocratic

* Haberl, *Bausteine für Musikgeschichte*, Band III.

act on the part of the Pope was against the usual
custom and was sure, for that reason, to be
secretly resented by the members of one of the
most jealous and exclusive bodies in Europe.
There were also actual disqualifications. Firstly,
Pierluigi was a married man, although, according
to the regulations, celibates only were eligible ;
secondly, there are reasons for believing that he
possessed but an indifferent singing-voice ; and
lastly, it was usual for members of the Pontifical
Choir to take ecclesiastical orders.

As Julius himself revised the rules of
admittance to the Choir, he must necessarily
have known very well what he was doing, and,
indeed, there was a saving clause in the regulations which permitted him to make exceptions
at his good pleasure. Thus he was justified in
using his prerogative. Probably for that reason
the Pontifical Choir dared to make no protest at
the time, and Pierluigi certainly thought himself
perfectly safe as this was a life-appointment. But
his enemies were soon to have him at their
mercy, for the Pope's days were numbered.

With shaken health, afflicted with gout, dis-
heartened by a long series of untoward political
circumstances which, being powerless to avert, he
had even aggravated by a lack of statesmanship,
of tact, and of self-command, Julius, for the last
portion of his life, withdrew himself more and

more from the cares of an office grown too heavy
for him, and spent much of his time in directing
the building operations of his new and exquisite
villa outside the Porta del Popolo, hard by the
Flaminian Way.* This was the so-called *Villa
di Papa Giulio,* begun in 1551, and finished three
years later. Designed by the famous Ticinese
architect, Vignola, it was surrounded by gardens
worthy of Eden.† Little wonder, then, that the
Pope sought there a refuge from mental and
physical ills. Who will doubt that he sent for
his singers, or that many a lovely madrigal floated
over the neighbouring heights of Monti Parioli
in the cool of a summer evening ?

But even these delights could not prolong the
life of the Pope. A return of his old enemy,
gout, for which an all too severe hunger-cure was
prescribed, brought his life to an end on March
23, 1555, after a short reign of five years.

In the midst of the turmoil and confusion
Pierluigi could have had but little time for
gauging his personal loss. But scarcely was the
Requiem Mass over with all its attendant ceremonies than his natural regret would be tempered
with renewed expectation, the Conclave electing
Cardinal Cervini as the succeeding Pontiff.‡ This

---

* Von Pastor. *Op. cit.*
  † The gardens were stocked with 38,000 fruit trees and adorned
with a nymphæum, exquisite statues, and fountains.
  ‡ April 9, 1555.

personage had already attracted the attention and admiration of his contemporaries through the saintliness of his life, by his gifts and aspirations ; in particular, great hopes were placed on him by the party for reform. Without entering deeply into the political history of this time, it may be useful to recall that the recent loss of England to the Papacy was regarded by the devout as a punishment inflicted on the Church for its laxity and worldliness, and as a clear warning of what was in store if the handwriting on the wall were disregarded. Thus the election of Cardinal Cervini was significant of the impending change and, with the passing of Julius, the spirit of the Renaissance, the worship of art, beauty, and culture, definitely waned.

To those so deeply concerned for the spiritual welfare of the Church, the election of Marcello Cervini doubtless seemed a direct answer to prayer. Endowed with great gifts, imbued with a passionate sense of the necessity for the purification of the Church, his succession to the Papacy was as if a purer air swept over Rome. An indirect confirmation of this statement may be found in the diary of one who regarded the change from a worldly point of view, and in commenting on the reforming zeal of the new Pope, observes, "everything is sad, gloomy, and funereal." Though the need for a purer atmosphere may be conceded in theory, in practice it is often a painful process.*

In the midst of the most weighty affairs connected with a world-jurisdiction difficult, to-day, to imagine, Marcellus yet found time for a matter very close to his heart. On Good Friday, on his return from that wonderful service in which the Reproaches create so poignant an effect, the Pope required that his choir should be summoned to his presence, and exhorted them to be careful, in future, that the music chosen was suitable for days of penitence and mourning ; also, that the words of the Mass were clearly distinguishable through the web of counter-point which embroidered the plainsong. Something like this has been heard before, and will no doubt be heard again ; but, in one respect, there is a remarkable advance to be noted. This may be said to be the first official recognition of Josquin's dictum, half a century earlier, that music must not only sound well, but mean something. Even the great Fleming, however, confined his discovery to setting the verse of a psalm in a motet, continuing to treat the Mass from a ceremonial point of view which took little account of the difference in re-ligious emotion implied between a *Kyrie eleison* and a *Gloria*. The Pope, therefore, in making such a recommendation to his choir, was instituting a new

* Quoted by Ranke.

standard in ecclesiastical music, and in so doing
revealed himself as a musician of singular insight,
insomuch that he insisted on the suitability of the
music chosen for Good Friday.*

This was certainly no mere coincidence. A
letter is in existence † which implies the Pope's
interest in the purity of the chant as far back as
1546. A man of the widest cultivation, it may
very well have struck him that music had not
yet taken its rightful place in the service of the
Sanctuary. Of all the Popes in whose reigns
Pierluigi's life-course was destined to run, not
one promised to work so beneficent an influence
on music and musicians as this singularly attractive personality Marcellus II.

As a member of the Pontifical Choir Pierluigi accompanied his colleagues into the Pope's
presence. Though, unfortunately, only the bare
mention of what took place has survived, it may
be surmised that the audience created a great
impression on at least one member of the Pontifical Choir, for the seed then sown was destined
to bear a world-famous fruit, the Mass of Pope
Marcellus, linking for ever the names of Pope
and musician.

But the Pope whose all-too-short reign

* Massarelli Angelo, Diarium Septimum : translated by Merkle,
Freiburg by Breslau, 1911.

† A letter, discovered by M. Dejob, from Cardinal Sirleto to
Cardinal Cervini.

created so extraordinary a spirit of hope and energy, whose very life seemed indispensable to the well-being of the Church, was taken from his labours after three weeks, and Christendom was again without a head. In the midst of the ferment caused by this event the Sacred College once more met and just twenty-three days after the death of Marcellus a new Pontiff was elected, on May 23, 1555, a date Pierluigi was to have every reason for remembering.

Cardinal Pietro Caraffa, who now assumed the tiara as Paul IV., while possessed of the same zeal for reform as his predecessor, conceived it from a different point of view. For instance, where it might be assumed that any peculiar or undeserved hardship created by his efforts in the sacred cause of reform would be mitigated by a man of such scrupulous and idealistic temperament as the highly cultivated Marcellus II., Paul, whose association with the dreaded Office of the Inquisition was little likely to temper with benevolence the natural severity of an unbending character, looked neither to right nor left but abode by the strict letter of the law, no matter what unmerited punishment might fall upon his victim. His incessant cry was "Reform, reform," with which, moreover, the Church had every reason to occupy herself, and one of his first activities was connected with the revision of the various offices in the Vatican ; thus setting his own house in order.

It may be that the Pope did not arrive without assistance at the discovery that all was not as it should be in the Pontifical Choir. The Puntatore's *absque consensu cantorum ingressus* (sic) *fuit* was possibly not alone inscribed in the records but graven on the hearts of the members of the Choir, and jealousy—like wine—improves with age. Besides, Pierluigi, a Roman, bade fair to outshine them all in reputation ; therefore the Pope's passion for reform might here be turned to advantage. Whether this be so or no—and there is yet another theory that Pierluigi's madrigals had offended the rigid temper of the Pope—his attention was called to the undeniable fact that the official number of the Choir had been exceeded, that three of its members were married men, and that one of them had been enrolled in defiance of the statute that a strict examination of the candidate should be conducted by the members of the Choir. The fiat went forth on July 30, 1555 ; Giovanni Pierluigi da Palestrina, and with him Leonardo Barré and Domenico Ferrabosco,* was to be dismissed from the Choir forthwith.

Against the injustice of this high-handed

* A member of that family bidden to the English Court, who there made music for a generation or two.

proceeding there was no redress. Ferrabosco's case was particularly hard, as he had relinquished a fine appointment in S. *Petronio*, the great Bolognese cathedral, to enter the Pontifical Choir. As we have seen, Pierluigi was there in accordance with the Pope's *motû proprio*, by the will of Julius III. himself, who framed the regulation he chose to disregard. The only sign of consideration for these hard cases shown by Paul was the intimation that a pension of six scudi would be paid monthly to the banished members, or a sum equal to two-thirds of their stipends.

The theory that madrigal-writing may have influenced the Pope's decision with regard to Pierluigi receives some support from the circumstance that both Ferrabosco and Barri were prolific writers of these things. Pierluigi, also, in this very year, published a collection of his own, though not a single copy of that edition has survived. There can be no doubt that to Paul IV. any connection between members of his own choir and compositions which set to music verse dealing with love and the beauty of women would appear to be little short of sacrilege, and some words which Pierluigi employs, later on, in a dedicatory address to Gregory XIII., lends colour to this view of the case. Be this as it may, Giovanni Animuccia, the Florentine whose history touches Pierluigi's at so many points, was installed in his place as member of the Pontifical Choir.

Pierluigi's situation was grave enough. He who had climbed the ladder of fame so rapidly now found himself again at the bottom. Without wishing to exaggerate the result of his dismissal it would surely be interpreted to his disadvantage. That Pierluigi himself so estimated his present circumstances seems evident, for the choir-attendance book of the Sixtine chapel records *Palestrina infirmus* from July 18 to July 30, on which date he was dismissed. Nor was he present at the official reading of the *motû proprio* at the meeting of the Chapter. At the same time, serious as the position was to a young man with wife and family, he must have remembered that he was already famous, and that to such as he a good appointment would not long be lacking. Nor was he without resources. It is probable he returned to Palestrina, " the place of cool breezes," until summer was over, there to recover his health and consider new plans. But nothing definite is known of him until his appointment as choirmaster to St. John Lateran, dated October 1, 1555. Baini says he hesitated to accept the new post until he was sure he would not lose his pension from the Pope.

According to the most recent researches, it does not appear that Pierluigi was invited to become choirmaster of St. John Lateran by the Canons, as Baini says, but by the Archpriest, Cardinal Ranuccio Farnese. There had been some irregularities in connection with the choir, and the Chapter placed the whole matter in the hands of Cardinal Farnese to deal with as he thought best. Possibly for that reason, not a single entry referring to Palestrina's nomination has been found, although in the book of accounts for 1555 occurs the following : " To Ms. Joannes, master of the choir, for his salary in the present month of October, scudi 6." * Further confirmation of the new appointment is to be found in the quaint memorandum : " for making the cotta of ms. Jo : master of the choir, of the aforesaid cortinella (stuff) b. 80." †

The present building of St. John Lateran hardly represents the church with which Pierluigi was familiar. Sharing with St. Peter's the proud distinction of dating its foundation from Constantine, it was at this moment in the state in which it was left by the restorations carried out by Popes Martin V. and Eugenius IV., so that neither the principal façade nor the entrance to the north transept were in existence. The pillars, too, of the interior were differently

---

* A Ms. Joanni maestro di cappella per il suo salario del presente mese d'ottobre scudi 6. Casimiri. G. P. da Palestrina.

† 80 bajocchi.

ordered, and the walls adorned with frescoes by
Gentile da Fabriano. There are two sketches
by Martin van Heemskerck, a pupil of Jan van
Scorel, who was in Rome from 1532 to 1535,
which represent the church as Pierluigi knew
it,* showing also the highly interesting remains
of the old palace of the *Laterani* on the east side
of the Basilica, once the residence of Constantine's
wife, Fausta, and given by him to the Popes,
who lived there until they migrated to Avignon.
There was the *Sancta Sanctorum*, the small Italo-
Gothic chapel of *S. Lorenzo in Palatio,* so-called
on account of its most venerated relics which
gave the entire precincts the sacro-sanct character
expressed in the inscription over the door : *Caput
Urbis Orbis Mundi Patriarchale et Imperiale.*

The choir of St. John Lateran had been
recently enlarged by Paul III., and endowed
by Cardinal de Cupis and was hardly of less
reputation than that of St. Peter's. In spite
of the temporary difficulties alluded to above,
it seems to have been the custom there to bestow
large gifts in money on the choirmaster and the
choristers, an agreeable proceeding the Chapter
wished, later on, to put a stop to. Pierluigi does
not appear to have taught the boys, which gives
rise to the supposition that he lived outside the

---

* Reproduced in *Die Stadt Rom zu Ende der Renaissance.*
L. v. Pastor.

PRINCIPAL FAÇADE OF S. GIOVANNI IN LATERANO BEFORE 1560, WHEN IT WAS ALTERED TO ITS PRESENT FORM.

Martin van Heemskerck

precincts. The warrant for this point of view lies in the Chapter-accounts from October, 1555, until the end of December (after which date the books are lost), which give the information that not Pierluigi but a certain Bernardino, tenor,* governed and instructed the boys.

The strong inclination of the new Pope towards austerity and discipline soon affected the moral atmosphere of Rome. As a famous historian puts it : † "Now they began once more to intone their *Confiteor* and *Credo*," inevitably turning Pierluigi's thoughts more persistently in the direction of Church music.

These years in St. John Lateran yielded two compositions which secured his reputation. These are the *Improperia* or Reproaches of our Lord, and a set of Lamentations ‡ taken from the Book of Lamentations.

It is certainly a matter for regret that Pope Marcellus did not live to hear the most poignant Good Friday music ever written. Previously, both the *Improperia* and the Lamentations were chanted to a plain-song melody. Pierluigi, with

---

* It has been suggested that this Bernardino was Pierluigi's brother. Until the present there is no proof. Monsignore Casimiri thinks it may have been a certain Bernardino, fellow chorister with Pierluigi in S. Maria Maggiore in 1537. G. P. da P., *Nuovi Documenti*.

† Ambros, *Geschichte der Musik*.

‡ His setting of the Latin hymn *Crux Fidelis* and some *Magnificats* also belong to this period.

his unerring instinct for apparent simplicity, the result of flawless technique, set them to a *faux-bourdon* or plain harmonization, of which the effect is unspeakably grand. Chanted during the ceremony of the Adoration of the Cross, it is difficult to suppose that these Reproaches could leave any hearer unmoved. *Popule meus, quid feci tibi ? aut in quo contristavi te ? responde mihi.*

The story runs that when the fame of this beautiful work reached him, the Pope desired to hear it sung. One cannot doubt there was here some small degree of compensation for the humiliation of being dismissed from the Pontifical Choir.

CHAPTER IV

THE chief Roman event of the year 1559 was the passing of Paul IV. (August 13). The Pope, whose hasty unbending character brought about some of the gravest crises the Church had yet encountered, was no more, the penitential season with its cleansing fires was to give place to a less exacting *régime*. Along with the rest of the Roman world, Pierluigi was probably braced and chastened by the rigours of a government which had nothing of the soft, luxurious Renaissance character. But the compositions belonging to this reign show in what spirit he had borne his disappointments and with what strength of character he set himself to repair his misfortunes. He had his personal reasons for regarding with anxiety any change in the Papacy; indeed, it is already obvious how much he had to gain or lose by the good disposition of the reigning Pontiff towards music and musicians, so it must not have been without a sense of satisfaction that he received the news of Cardinal Giovanni Angelo Medici's elevation to

the chair of St. Peter as Pius IV., whose artistic
tastes were well known and who was a warm
patron of music, taking especial interest in the
art of composition.*

To Pierluigi the practical and material side of
his profession was of the utmost importance. It
need hardly be said that the conditions of life in
a small town like Palestrina and in the great city
were absolutely different. In the Sabine Hills,
a small settled income, vines, and olives, probably
provided as many amenities as the circumstances
required, but now the exigencies of an official
position and a growing family pressed more
heavily upon the composer. It has been made
a subject of implied reproach that he was never
indifferent to the financial aspect of a question,
nor ever neglected an opportunity of attaching
himself to a wealthy patron ; but he should rather
be praised for precisely those qualities which
prove him to have been a good husband, careful
father, and prudent man, qualities—all of them—
by no means inseparable from genius. Moreover,
it is fairly obvious that he could never have
enriched the world with the extraordinarily large
number of his compositions had he not possessed
in a high degree the capacity for managing his
affairs, and thereby securing the necessary environment of calm and comparative ease for intellectual

* See Ambros, vol. iv. p. 18.

labours. The honied phrases of his dedications
were the usual custom,* and even in our own
day not entirely unknown, and it has been wittily
said that a powerful patron might be considered
in the light of a policeman, by means of whom it
was possible to redress one's private wrongs, and
make headway against one's enemies. Possibly
he was not altogether satisfied with the financial
conditions of his new post, in spite of the four
barrels of wine which, according to the accounts,
he sold to the authorities of St. John Lateran in
July, 1559, for eight golden scudi ! † At all events,
whatever the reason, after five years of office he
left St. John Lateran so hurriedly that the secretary to the Chapter thinks it right to emphasise
the speed of his departure.‡ This curiously
worded document, so recently discovered,§ runs
as follows :—

Cum Domini Canonici alias ad res cappellae
cantorum administrandas deputati retulerint,
et D. Io: Petrum Loysium magistrum dictae
cappellae unà cum filio penè improuiso
abscessisse, et per ipsos Canonicos
id illi facile licuisse, eoquod noluerit
decreto proximi superioris Capituli stare,
Ne quid scilicet ei pro uictu cuiuslibet ex
pueris, ultra Julios 25 quolibet mense daretur,

---

* See the Preface to the Bible of James I. for a notable example.
† Casimiri, *Nuovi documenti biografici*, 1918.
‡ Idem.   § Idem.

Omnes id una uoce ratum habuerunt, eandemque
Canonicorum deputationem confirmarunt
qui alium in ipsius d. Jo : locum perquirant
et inuentum admittant.

The date of this is August 3, 1560, and it
is preceded by two others, dated respectively
July 20 and 27, which may, or may not, throw
some light on Pierluigi's hasty departure, for
they refer to economies in the management of
the choir. The great musician shows here some
evidence of an embittered and irritable state of
mind. Even if not prepared to accept the new
financial conditions, it hardly seems in keeping
with his customary prudence to throw up such
a position with no other in prospect, and it is
possible that there was some other motive behind.
Still neither the Chapter nor Pierluigi appear to
have nourished a permanent grievance in the
matter, as will be seen later.

The intervening six months before Pierluigi
returned to the church in which he had been a
chorister twenty-four years earlier, are in our
present state of knowledge a blank. It can only be
guessed that much of the time was given to certain
glorious compositions which were shortly to make
their appearance. The Chapter decree above
refers to Pierluigi's son,* already a chorister, and
about ten years old at this time. Later evidence

* Ridolfo.

will show that he with his brothers was carefully trained in counterpoint and the playing of various instruments, and Pierluigi may have devoted this *interregnum* to his family.

In the *Atti Capitolari* of *S. Maria Maggiore* against the date March 1, 1561, is to be read the ratification of Pierluigi's appointment to the *Basilica Liberiana* (*S. Maria Maggiore*).* His connection with it as choirmaster was destined to coincide with a very brilliant period of his life. The pleasant fancy may perhaps be permitted that his genius was spurred to fresh exertions by the classic beauty of his environment. One of the oldest in that city of old churches, *S. Maria Maggiore* took high rank as one of the four patriarchal churches, the other three being St. Peter's, St. John Lateran, and St. Paul Outside the Walls, all of them churches within whose parochial boundaries the whole of the human race is included. In other words, their parishioners consisted of the faithful irrespective of nationality. The miraculous story of its foundation (under Pope Liberius) fixes the date of the earliest building little later than the reign of Constantine. It was re-erected in the fifth century by Sixtus III., to which remote time the magnificent nave adorned with mosaics is assigned. In Pierluigi's time neither the splendid Sixtine nor Borghese Chapels were erected, otherwise the

* Casimiri, *op. cit.*

general aspect of the church can have changed little.

As far as is known Pierluigi had the choristers under his charge in his new post. That is to say, his stipend depended on their number. As a great deal of discussion has been aroused by a sentence in his dedicatory address to a later Pope, it may be well to make some inquiry at this point into the amount of his present income.

His monthly salary in S. Maria Maggiore amounted at first to thirteen, later, sixteen scudi on the addition of another chorister to the three already in his charge, in all about one hundred and ninety-two scudi.* For this sum Pierluigi was expected to feed the boys and give them musical instruction. That is to say, he received six scudi as salary, and two scudi and a half per head for each chorister. As quarters in the precincts were always assigned to the members of the choir, there would be no expenditure necessary for housing. Presents were customary after the great festivals of the Church. As we have already seen, these became so costly that the Chapter of St. John Lateran desired to check the practice. To these sources of income must be added Pierluigi's pension as ex-member of the Pontifical choir, amounting to a yearly sum of approximately fifty-eight pounds. Then comes an uncertain sum

---

* At present-day value, about £156 per annum.

for dedications to rich patrons—habitual at the time—and the organization of music for occasions festive or mournful. The present was an epoch in which men of wealth and position desired to pose as excellent musicians, so that there were always compositions to be corrected and put into shape, or lessons to give. Of professional pupils an account will be given later. According to the custom of the times these lived in the master's house and became part of his family. As has already been seen, Pierluigi had property and turned it to practical account. A year or two later this was to be added to by the death of his father, and until the close of his own life, documentary evidences of the acquisition of small pieces of property show that this tended to increase. Presumably these facts were unknown to the Abbé Baini when he deplores so bitterly the poverty of the great musician. He was certainly not rich, but, all things considered, his income compares not unfavourably with many a Church musician of high repute to-day. It will be necessary to return to this subject later.

In this period the Abbé Baini places the romantic story that in many of the older biographies would seem to form Pierluigi's chief claim to the veneration of posterity. Increased knowledge has, however, thrown a new light on his place in musical history, one certainly not less

great but more logical. One of the recurring
quarrels referred to in the introductory chapter
between musicians and clergy led to the intervention
of Pope Pius IV., who finally decided to place the
matter before the Council of Trent along with
many others affecting Church discipline. According to Baini's version, the dispute was so sharp
that the Churchmen proposed to exclude music
altogether from the Office of the Mass; whereupon Pierluigi stepped in and effected the rescue
of Church music by the composition of three
masses so blameless, so transcendently beautiful,
that the Pope compared them to the music of the
heavenly spheres. That Pierluigi was capable of
the feat no one would wish to deny, but the story
as it stands cannot be substantiated in its details.

There is not a shadow of doubt, however, that
the clergy did complain and with reason. One
such remonstrance has survived. It is from the
Bishop of Ruremonde, who states that after giving
the closest attention he had been unable to
distinguish one word sung by the choir.* Nor
was this the only cause of complaint. The use of
secular melodies by the titles of which the masses
themselves were not infrequently referred to, as
well as the interpolation of non-canonical text,†
were entirely justifiable grievances. Members of

---

* Ambros, *Geschichte der Musik.*
† Or tropes.

the extreme party *may* have been of opinion that
the only remedy was to do away with music in the
service of the Church, or at all events to confine
it within the limits of the ancient plain-song ;
one of the difficulties being that what was done
and done well in the chief churches was marred by
miserable execution of other choirs working under
less favourable circumstances. As conformity was
sought after as a matter of principle, it seemed
safer to return to the ancient simplicity rather
than to endeavour to bring the bad up to the level
of the good. But it is certain that the friends of
music would have intervened to protect it from
such a drastic course.

The affair aroused the deepest interest. Many
of the delegates to the Council applied previously
to their over-lords for advice. The Legate to
the Emperor Ferdinand I. followed this course
and received a reply which shows a very pretty
sense of discrimination on the Emperor's part.
If the Church excluded sentimental music (*mollior
harmonia*) let her retain figured music which so
often awakens the spirit of piety. The significa-
tion of *mollior harmonia* is taken as a reference to
the practice, just then coming into vogue, of
modernizing the ancient modes or scales by the
employment of accidentals (known as *musica ficta*)
in order to soften the asperities of awkward
intervals. The figured music referred to was

obviously the highly organized counterpoint of
the great masters of the time. The Council's
verdict at the historic twenty-second sitting does
not support Baini's account : *ab ecclesiis musicas
eas, ubi sive organo, sive cantu, lascivum aut
impurum aliquid miscetur arceant, item sæculares
omnes actiones vana atque adeo profana colloquia,
ut Domus Dei vere domus orationis esse videatur ac
dici possit :* thus, instead of debating the banish-
ment of music they declare it must be purified
from the secular spirit, from anything profane ;
and in the twenty-fourth sitting the subject
comes up again, when the prohibition of *mollior
harmonia* is recommended.   This mild ruling was
in the best interests of musicians and clergy, for
the new and dangerous secular spirit was gaining
ground rapidly in Venice and Florence.   At the
same time, the Council were not reactionary.
Figured music, which, as the Emperor Ferdinand
pertinently remarked, so often awakened the spirit
of piety, was not to be interfered with.   Curiously
enough, there is a strong likeness between this
ruling and the words used by Pope John XXII.
in a thirteenth-century dispute between clergy and
musicians.   Then, as now, it was suggested by the
clergy that the best way to overcome the difficulty
was a return to the ancient melodies, and the Pope
interposed to save the rude harmonies then in use
because in his opinion they assisted devotion.

Shortly afterwards Pius IV. appointed a committee to see that the general reforms enjoined by the Council of Trent were carried into effect. This was composed of eight Cardinals, of whom two were deputed to attend to the resolutions affecting music. Pope Pius, "the friend of music," showed his sympathy with its cause by appointing his nephew, Cardinal Carlo Borromeo, in whose judgment he notoriously placed great reliance, and Cardinal Vitellozzi Vitelli, both young men of great energy of character and passionate lovers of music. These entered on their task in a tactful and sensible manner. Instead of peremptory injunctions as to what should or should not be done, they called together eight Papal singers to consider the question, showing that they realized reform must be undertaken with the co-operation of the musicians themselves and not as punitive measures against them. At the first meeting a decision was easily reached that masses with secular themes should be banned, as, also, the interpolation of unauthorized text (tropes). But when Borromeo insisted that the words sung in the office of the Mass should be intelligible, the singers declared that this was impossible ; whereupon the Cardinal pointed out this was not so, for Pierluigi's *Improperia* and Costanzo Festa's *Te Deum* were instances to the

contrary.* It is probable that Cardinal Borromeo
had also in mind Pierluigi's Hexachord Mass, the
theme of which was constructed on the first six
notes of the scale. This was dedicated to the Pope
in the preceding year (so what becomes of Baini's
romance ?) and through its admirable balance of
sound forms an excellent illustration of the
argument. It may indeed be assumed that
Pierluigi's advice had already been sought as to
the best means of carrying out the Council of
Trent's recommendations, as it must have been
long before seen that the future of Church music
was in his hands. At that moment he was in the
full tide of inspiration, and besides the Hexachord
Mass—an example of the desired limpidity and
containing a glorious *Pleni* for two sopranos and
altos—there is some ground for believing one of
the most famous of his works was already in
existence in manuscript form, the celebrated Mass
of Pope Marcellus. Moreover, a book of motets
had already appeared, so what becomes of Baini's
so-called Rescue of Church music ? †

* The choir attendance-book notes, against April 28, 1565, that
the Pontifical singers met together in the house of Cardinal Vitelli
to sing certain masses before him so that he might hear if the text
was distinct. (*Geschichte der Päpste*, Bd. vii.) The Jesuit de
Cressolles relates he heard from a third person that Pierluigi himself
said Pius IV. had withdrawn his opposition to church music on
account of his (P.'s) masses.
† This was the first book of motets, dedicated to Cardinal
Ridolfo Pio, and published in 1563, though not a single copy of
this early edition has been found.

JOANNES PETRALOYSIUS PRAENESTINUS
Imago secundum prototypum in Archivo Musico Basilicae Vaticanae conservatum
By kind permission of Messrs. Breitkopf and Härtel)

A pause may here conveniently be made to consider the above-mentioned motets, which mark an interesting phase in Pierluigi's development.

Custom permitted a greater freedom in the composition of the motet than in the mass, and modern influences were not so rigorously excluded. As the text was taken from the Bible or the Breviary the words of the mass were not in question, and the Church therefore saw no reason to interfere. The rise of the motet coincides with the dawn of the Netherlands School and already, at Josquin's hands, it received its final shape, the essential details changing little hereafter. But though the form, that of a *cantus firmus* accompanied by other voices in graceful florid counterpoint, changed little, it grew gradually to resemble the madrigal in inspiration, as one sister in the cloister may resemble another in the world. There was no attempt made at dramatic illustration of the text, but the music annotated the words, often to the extent of an attractive ingenuousness. The closeness of the weaving gets richer as Pierluigi advances in life, and the quality becomes more ecstatic, more fervent.* For example, there is a passage in *O admirabile*

---

* Generalization is difficult if it be borne in mind that the variety was practically inexhaustible, the text being drawn from so many sources.

commercium where the voices poise on the exclama-
tion, as if unable from sheer wonder and awe to
proceed, as if transfixed before a beatific vision ;
and in the subsequent *alleluja* there is such a
jubilation as though the joy were too great for
articulation and the air became filled with short
emotional ejaculations. Not infrequently the
association of words and music was obtained
through the selection of a theme from the plain-
song melody for the day on which that portion
of Scripture was read. Or one word, such as
" holiness " or " praise " received a particular
tone-colouring, or quality of sound, each time it
recurred, thus impressing it on the mind of the
listener and giving it significance. Like all the
really great masters, Pierluigi concealed the art
of his methods by employing an apparent
simplicity, in other words, the art of concealing
art. It is possible that he did, as Baini suggests,
owe something to Costanzo Festa, who combined
clearness of structure and expressiveness with the
most learned contrapuntal dexterity and device,—
Dr. Burney quotes his motet *Quam pulchra es,
anima mea* as a model of its kind,—but the fact
will always remain that what Pierluigi learnt at
the hands of his predecessors and contemporaries
he transmuted to a more precious metal.

It is pleasant to think, whether justifiably or
not, that Pope Marcellus on the historic Good

Friday of his short reign turned Pierluigi's attention to the sincerity and homogeneity of words with music which marks that composer's masterpieces. In that case, and the supposition is by no means far-fetched, the great Mass of Pope Marcellus was a recognition and a homage. Not only the general consensus of opinion but also the composer's own conviction agree that he reached in this work a more absolute expression of the ideal than any of his predecessors or contemporaries, and, in the dedication, his phrase *novo modorum genere* (of a new species of melodies) might be interpreted as showing him aware of the fact. It was only published in the second volume of the masses, *Liber Secundus*, in the year 1567 but certainly existed in manuscript as early as 1564, to which year experts assign the oldest existing copy, that belonging to the library of *S. Maria Maggiore*. As an example of the unassuming manner in which this masterpiece stole upon the world, it may be mentioned that copy bears no title whatever, and it is therefore impossible to decide whether this was accidentally omitted or whether it was added as an afterthought. Before stopping to consider this beautiful work in greater detail, it will be well to mention the rest of the masses contained in *Liber Secundus*. These were five in number :—*De Beata Virgine ; Aspice Domine ; Salvum me fac ; Inviolata ;* and *Ad fugam.* As

is pointed out by Ambros, the last-named is
not fugal in character but the voices sing in
perpetual canon. Its inclusion in the second
book of masses was as if Pierluigi wished to
heighten the contrast between old and new
methods and to show in what direction music
tended.

The introductory portion of the *Missa Papae
Marcelli* is written in the hypolydian mode with
occasional incursion to the mixolydian. Beginning on the fifth it rises to the highest note of
the mode, sweeping down to its final (C) and
beyond. But nothing in this fragment of analysis
could possibly convey to the reader the exquisite
balance and repose of the opening phrase. It is
like a benediction, quietening the spirit with a
heavenly sense of peace ; or it suggests a vision
of the white wings of a dove folding as they come
to earth. The short phrases forming the points
of imitation seem not so much contrapuntal
devices as passages of sheer inevitability. There
is no sense of effort ; the melodies shift and
intermingle as if without design, but always
forming harmonies which satisfy the mind beyond
all telling. Perhaps the most striking feature is
simplicity. In the score the erudition must
astonish, but in performance the voices blend so
naturally they impress the hearer with a sense of
fortuitous confluence. The entire mass is written

within the compass of two octaves and a fifth, but never for a moment is the ear wearied by so small a range. The absence of mechanical rhythm, or a strong or weak beat arbitrarily applied, permits a pure unbroken flow of sound and the sense of a calm, sweet, ordered progress, only interrupted as the voices rest on their allotted points of repose. In the *Credo* the choice of phrase is extraordinarily expressive, but it is in the *Sanctus* that Pierluigi reaches that fullness of sound, that suave harmony transfiguring the words as a nimbus adorns the pure, pale face of a saint. Extremely simple in design, it is full of little scale-passages, joyous flights of melodies suggesting the angels in a Fra Angelico fresco. This multiplication of similes may at least serve to show the imagination and idealism the master here displays. Such an experience tranquillizes and relieves the spirit, and the four-part Benedictus suggests the sending of an earthly embassy on high with a message of thankfulness and praise. Once again, it must be insisted that the apparent simplicity marks the perfection of the achievement, the plasticity of the material won after endless toil. Considered from this point of view, the old Netherlanders with their compound time-measurements, their canons and all the rest of their diabolical in-genuities, *all* had a hand in the *Missa Papae Marcelli* though the master-mind was necessary

to divine the ultimate end. If to-day this mass
can still work its wondrous spell on the jaded
senses of the modern musician, what must have
been its effect in the sixteenth century, in all
the freshness of its revelation ? Those heavenly
harmonies surely seemed little short of miraculous
as they echoed through that marvellous nave in
S. Maria Maggiore, or down the five aisles of old
St. Peter's.*

* The transverse wall already divided the old building into two.
See pages 160-161.

CHAPTER V

THE death of Pius IV. occurred in 1565, the year in which he appointed Cardinal Carlo Borromeo, his nephew, with Cardinal Vitellozzi Vitelli supervisors of the reforms enjoined by the Council of Trent. Pierluigi thus lost a generous perceptive patron who had raised his pension * as ex-member of the Pontifical Choir by thirty-six scudi annually. He was certainly not alone in regretting the late Pope, for in his successor Rome was to possess a Pontiff whose remarkable ascetism, as well as passionate devotion to the spiritual welfare of the Church allowed no time for, or interest in, matters of less gravity. It was obviously an affair of deep importance to musicians whether, or no, the Head of Christendom deigned to take an interest in Church music. Even if only within the limits of Rome itself (and it is clear that the field would be as wide as the domain of the Church) the tastes of a music-loving Pope

* In consideration of past or future compositions for the use of the Pontifical Choir.

must be respected, and he must be received
on his periodical visitations to the individual
churches with the choicest music the circumstances afforded. Probably there was considerable rivalry in this respect, to the great benefit of
the musicians. It is a phenomenon not confined
to any particular age or place, and no art is more
dependent on its environment.

Like Julius III., delighting in splendid entertainments, Pius IV. was the last of the Popes to
exhibit that love of art which characterized the
periods of the Renaissance. This is abundantly
apparent in Rome, for he takes high rank amongst
the building pontiffs of the sixteenth century.
But it was becoming increasingly evident that the
great days of architecture were over, that a change
n artistic formulas was at hand, classical yielding
to baroque, with a craving for dramatic expression
which ignored the inherent limitations of the
material employed. The spirit of music was not
destined to escape the influence, though the effects
only made themselves apparent later. This was
a foregone conclusion, for it follows that when a
point of perfection has been reached in a certain
direction, no further progress along the same lines
is possible, and " old lamps " must be " exchanged
for new." The result in this instance was the
creation of opera, a logical development of the
growth of personality. The first step in this

direction was the expansion of orchestral accompaniment, though at present this was a purely secular development and did not invade the precincts of the Church to any extent before the end of the century. Thus Pierluigi was more fortunate than his great contemporary, Michelangelo, who, denied the happiness of completing the new church to San Pietro, felt his long life all too short. The musician put the finishing touches to his structure and died before the sweeping changes brought about by time. There is, by the way, no record that these two men were acquainted, but they can scarcely have escaped meeting on the common ground of their activities, and no more fruitful study for a picture of Pierluigi's environment can be made than that of the literature built round the tall saturnine figure in black satin doublet which, about this time, for ever disappeared from the streets of Rome.*

Still, nothing affected the speed of Pierluigi's pen. In 1570 *Liber Tertius* came from the press. The titles of the eight masses it contained are : *Spem in alium ; Primi toni ; Missa brevis ; De Feria* —these for four voices ; *L'homme armé;* and *Repleatur os meum,* for five. The two remaining

---

* It may perhaps here be recalled that Pierluigi set to music words by Michelangelo's friend, the exquisite lady, Vittoria Colonna, a slight thread of connection between the three personages consisting in the fact that Pierluigi was vassal of the Colonna family, who were probably not unaware of his remarkable genius.

masses are for six voices : *De beata Virgine,** and
the famous Hexachord Mass inscribed to Pius IV.
in 1562, the Crucifixus and Pleni of which are
acknowledged examples of Pierluigi's most angelic
style. Without stopping to analyse it the student's
attention may be drawn to the interesting employment of the sixth (hexachord) continually pro-
gressing up and down, a mechanical device which
in no way hinders the flow or the unusual
simplicity of effect. By the grouping of the voices
Pierluigi produces the illusion of antiphonal
choirs.†

Perhaps it has already been observed that the
third volume contains a ‚mass with a secular title,
and this notwithstanding the Council of Trent's
prohibition, the words running : " Music must
be purified from the secular spirit, from anything
profane." How is this injunction to be reconciled
with a mass written on the theme of a popular
song ? The answer may be sought in the
distinction between the spirit and the letter. As
was already pointed out, in speaking of the mass
Ecce Sacerdos Magnus, it was a sheer impossibility
for the listener to detect the theme in the web of
enveloping counterpoint. To the end of his life
Pierluigi continued to select his *cantus firmus*

* The former version in *Liber Secuudus* is for four voices.
† It may be permitted to recall in this connection the antiphonal
choirs S. Ignatius (1st century, A.D.) heard in his Vision of the
Divine Birth.

where it pleased him ; usually calling his mass by a non-committal title, such as *Sine Nomine* (Without Name) or *Primi Toni* (In the First Tone) so that the proprieties were observed. But the mass entitled *L'homme armé* was openly avowed, for the celebrated theme had become consecrated by custom to such a use. Seventeen masses before Pierluigi's day were already written round the melody, and these by the most celebrated musicians of their time. The composer is unknown, but Dufay was the first to use the theme and thus started it on its notable career, for which reason the suggestion has been made—on rather slender grounds—that Busnois, his pupil, was the author. On the other hand, Dr. Burney attempted to identify it with one of the oldest traditional songs, the *Chanson de Roland*. The mystification was increased by finding a sort of trick-composition, made up of the first sections of three separate tunes, a practice to which the musical humorists of that time were much addicted, and known as Quodlibet, Fricassée, Pot-pourri, or Coq-à-l'asne.* The words associated with these and strung together reading thus—

> L'homme, l'homme armé
> Hé ! Robinet, tu m'as le mort donné
> Quand tu t'en vas.

—the want of correspondence between mood and

* Brenet in *Vie de Palestrina.*

tense remaining either unperceived or being set down to the inaccurate writing of the time. The first section alone of the tune was that identified with the words *L'homme armé*, the second line was proved to be the first of a song in an MS. now in the *Bibliothèque Nationale* in Paris, with its proper context, and thus the riddle was solved.* The third line has not yet been identified.

As Dufay was the greatest master of his time, it became a matter of self-respect with succeeding musicians to employ this theme and to accompany it with every conceivable learned device ; in short, a species of self-imposed thesis. Josquin wrote two, † " a Netherlandish composition through and through, but also one of his most magnificent, a really monumental work." Pierluigi worked on it twice ; on the first occasion, as we have seen, taking no trouble to disguise it ; on the second, simply giving his mass the title of *Missa Quarta*. The whole of Pierluigi's Church compositions stand as witnesses that he not only succeeded in abolishing " anything profane," but found a new and ideal expression beyond any expectation the Council of Trent could have formulated. It may therefore be assumed this was the reason that his continued use of secular themes (to be regarded as so much

* By Michel Brenet, *Vie de Palestrina.*
† Ambros in *Geschichte der Musik.*

technical raw material) escaped censure from the authorities. This, at least, is a pardonable hypothesis. Yet another mass in the same volume is based on a secular theme. This is the one entitled *Primi toni*, and founded on a madrigal by Pierluigi's former companion in misfortune, Domenico Ferrabosco, of which the first line is "Je suis son giovanetta." Only a few weeks before his death, in the last book sent to the press, Pierluigi included a mass founded on a French song "Je suis deshéritée," the secular words still existing through the curious circumstance that a French composer, by name Jean Maillard, in a mass on the same theme published at Paris in 1552, put the secular words under the liturgical in order * that his ingenious manipulation of the theme might not escape notice. Little wonder, then, that the supposition arose, centuries later, that choirs were so lost to all sense of decency as to sing the secular words during the solemn function of the Mass itself.

About this time there are indications of a certain restlessness, as if Pierluigi considered the advisability of obtaining some lucrative and congenial post in one or other of the numerous Courts in his own land or elsewhere. The changed conditions of the Pontifical Court probably counted for something in this, or the

* Again Brenet.

example of his celebrated contemporary, Orlando di Lassus, may have had its weight. It were but human if the Roman observed with envy the superb editions which through the generosity of his patron, Duke Albert of Bavaria, the Netherlander was able to issue from time to time. Whether or no Pierluigi sighed for a princely Maecenas who would release him from financial anxieties, and regard his work as conferring lustre on his reign, it is certain that the second and third volumes of masses were dedicated to one of the most prominent monarchs in Europe, His Most Catholic Majesty, Philip II. of Spain. According to Baini, this was at the request of the Spanish Cardinal, Pacheco, acting either on his own initiative, or because he had received a hint that such a dedication would not be unpleasing to his royal master. If so, Pierluigi was justified in hoping for a brilliant appointment to the Court of Spain, and there was much in favour of such a step. The dignity and religious emotion of this most interesting school of composition are proof enough that Pierluigi would have been sure of the recognition and sympathy due to his genius. But Philip apparently contented himself with a bare message of thanks, and between the publication of *Liber Secundus* and *Liber Tertius* a new and celebrated name appears in the chronicle. It was already known that in Cardinal Ippolito

d'Este Pierluigi found a patron: so much
was certain from the dedication to the volume
of motets which appeared in 1569. He refers
there to great benefits received. One of the
most princely figures of the late Renaissance,
Cardinal Ippolito d'Este was a son of the Duke
of Ferrara by his wife, Lucrezia Borgia, and to
the advantages of his birth and position were
added accomplishments quite in keeping with the
traditions of the period. A man of enormous
wealth, he built the famous villa at Tivoli, and
among the palaces he possessed elsewhere, that
situated on the Quirinal Hill in Rome was
famous for the number and beauty of the ancient
Greek and Roman statues collected there. Nor
were his artistic tastes centred on plastic forms
alone. It is recorded that, entrusted with highly
delicate and important diplomatic missions to the
Court of France in 1561 as Papal Legate, he
took with him not only four hundred horsemen,
but, what is more to the present purpose, his
private choir.*

In Cardinal d'Este, then, Pierluigi might
expect to find both an appreciative and generous
patron. Although still holding his office in
S. Maria Maggiore he seems to have obtained
permission to absent himself from his duties there

---

* L. von Pastor, *Geschichte der Päpste,* vol. vii.

during the three hot months of summer. The entries to that effect in the expenses of the Este household for 1564 are conclusive.* Evidently it was a satisfactory arrangement on both sides, for in August, 1567, Pierluigi returned to the Cardinal's service, remaining there until the end of March, 1571. His salary was at the annual rate of 79 *scudi romani*, 20 *bajocchi*, and the expenses of his living were at the Cardinal's charge. Thus it was a permanent appointment with a yearly agreement. It is to be hoped that further documents will at some time or other throw light on this interesting period of the great composer's life. Slight as the information is, it is corroborated by other entries in the books of *S. Maria Maggiore* and, strangely enough, of the Lateran. After his return from the first engagement with the Cardinal he figures—in January, 1565—as witness to a legal document in the archives of the first-named basilica, there styled : *Jo: Petro Aloysio alias Giannetto da Prenestina magistro cappello* ; a proof that he remained, in spite of his absence, attached to the church. But it is not possible to suppose that he retained his office there during his four years in the Cardinal's service, and as there is evidence that he was at St. John Lateran in Holy Week (1567), it certainly

* G. Campori, *Delle relazione di Orlando di Lasso e di Pier Gio. da Palestrina co` principi estensi,*

seems as if he had already left *S. Maria Maggiore* some months before he entered upon his second period of service with the Cardinal. As has been justly pointed out,* it is most improbable that any church would consent to forego the services of its choirmaster in favour of another church at such a time as Holy Week. The entry in the books of *S. Giovanni in Laterano* has a delightful quaintness. It runs : "*A di XII. detto per un paro di capretti donati a Ms Gio : da pelestrina per ordine del R. do S.r Attilio Cecio per haverci aggiutato la settimana santa*, bj. 90."† This gift in kind reminds us that Pierluigi still had property in Palestrina, to which place it is possible the goats were consigned.

But it is evident that Pierluigi still cherished thoughts of an appointment at some great foreign Court, and this although he had returned for the second time to his service with Cardinal d'Este. A document ‡ from the State Archives in Vienna shows this plainly. It is from the Ambassador Arco to His Majesty Maximilian II. and runs : "*Il cantore Giov. di Palestrina si contenta di venir a servire la M^{tà} V^{ra} per quattro cento scudi d'oro*

---

* Casimiri, *op cit.*

† Trans. : "On the 12th given for a pair of goats presented to M. Gio da Pelestrina (*sic*) by order of the most Rev. Sir Attilio Cecio for having assisted in Holy Week, 80 bajocchi."

‡ Given by Dr. Ludwig von Pastor in *Geschite der Päpste*, vol. viii. p. 152.

*l'anno ; io ho fatto quanto ho potuto per ridurlo
ancora a meno, ma non ho potuto ottener più. Adesso
aspetterò che la M^{tà} V^{ra} mi commandi quello ho a
fare circa quest' huomo, il quale mi vien lodato da
molti.*"

Or :

"The singer (*sic*) Giov. di Palestrina is content
to come and serve your Majesty for 400 gold scudi
yearly. I have done what I could to reduce it to
less, but have not been able to obtain more.
Now I await your Majesty's commands what I
am to do respecting this man who is praised to
me by many."

But something intervened, for on January 3,
1568, the laconic notice from Arco runs : " *Con
Giov. di Palestrina non passerò più innanzi ;* " or :
" With Giov. di Palestrina I shall not go further,"
and whether there is any connection between
these letters and a new development in Pierluigi's
life-history is not at present elucidated. William
of Gonzaga, Duke of Mantua, whose wife was
a daughter of the Emperor Ferdinand I., and consequently sister to the Emperor Maximilian II.,
here enters into the chronicle.

Until this moment there has been little to
depend upon in the attempt to present Pierluigi's
life and character in relation to his environment.
Now, however, comes a remarkable series of letters
not hitherto translated into English, which were dis-

covered in the Mantuan archives by the Abbé *Pietro Canal*, who published them in his work entitled, *Della musica in Mantova, notizie, tratte principalmente dell' archivio Gonzaga*. The importance of them is such that it is, indeed, not too much to say that without these letters Pierluigi's personality would have remained sealed to the present generation. As it is, his relations with the Duke not only show the estimation in which the musician was held, but also give valuable indications of his opinions. Some of the letters were translated into German,* and their original number has been added to through later researches.† These Mantuan records are certainly some of the most rich in detail that we possess of life in the sixteenth and seventeenth centuries.

The letters begin early in the year 1568 and continue to within a short time of Pierluigi's death. Most of them were personally exchanged, a few are written, at the Duke's request, by members of his *entourage*. Before proceeding to consider them at length it may be as well to remind the reader of the pains the reigning princes were at, to increase the splendour of their courts by the enlightened protection of the arts. This largerly accounts for the peregrinations of artists almost always at this period a feature of their

* By Dr. Haberl.
† See Bertolotti, *I a Musica in Mantova*.

life-history. It was quite the usual course to send the master of a choir on a journey through Europe in order to collect good singers for his lord's chapel, and an apposite instance of this is preserved to us by one Massimo Trajano. It refers to the Duke of Bavaria, the most generous patron of Orlando di Lassus.*

"The Duke, seeing that his predecessor's chapel was far beneath his own ideal, sent messages and letters, with gifts and promises, through all Europe to select learned musicians and singers with fine voices and experience. And it came to pass that in a short time he had collected as great a number of *virtuosi* as he could possibly attain, chosen from all the musicians in Germany and other countries by his composer the excellent Orlando di Lasso." There were other, and nefarious, ways of compassing the same end, for— in the history of Lassus himself—it is related that, as a young boy and the possessor of a singularly beautiful voice, he was stolen three times ; on the last occasion finding himself *nolens volens* in the service of a Gonzaga, Viceroy of Italy.

The Court of Mantua, in particular, cultivated music with both ardour and generosity, and Duke William of Gonzaga remained throughout the rest of his life a faithful and fervent admirer of

* Written variously as Orlando di Lasso, or Roland de Lattre.

Pierluigi's genius. Succeeding to the Dukedom at the age of fourteen, he was under the tutelage of his uncle, the highly cultivated Cardinal Ercole Gonzaga. After his marriage to the Emperor's daughter, his Court became famous for its brilliance, and he spared no pains to attract thither the finest singers and instrumentalists. Extremely desirous of getting the best possible material for the Church of St. Barbara, built and endowed by himself, he commissioned his choirmaster, Giaches Wert,* himself an excellent Flemish musician and an interesting personality, to obtain a mass from Pierluigi. A letter, dated February, 1568, acquaints us with the result, After the many compliments custom demanded Pierluigi informs the Duke that the mass is ready which his "rare musician Messer Giaches" had asked for, and it is herewith despatched—if it does not come up to expectation he hopes he will be allowed to try again, when the Duke must tell him whether he desires a long or a short mass, and whether he is very particular that the words should be clearly heard.† The answer to this letter is dated April 19, addresses the musician as *Messer Giovanni Pietro Luigi da Palestina* (sic), and contains

---

* Sometimes written "Jachet."

† The first section of this sentence may be taken to apply to the difference between a highly ceremonial mass and one for ordinary occasions ; the latter section was probably an attempt to find out whether the Duke preferred the old or new school of composition.

an assurance from the Duke that his delay in
thanking Pierluigi for the mass is not because he
did not like it—on the contrary, it pleases him
extremely, and as a proof thereof he has desired a
certain Fiera to demonstrate this ; from which it
may reasonably be inferred that Cavaliere Fiera
acted as the Duke's purse-bearer on this occasion.
At any rate, on May 1, a letter was written by
Pierluigi to the Duke in which he expresses his
warmest gratitude for the gift of fifty ducats and
reiterates his earnest wish to serve him per-
petually.

On July 31 of this year Scipio Gonzaga, a
kinsman of the Duke (who became Patriarch of
Jerusalem and subsequently Cardinal, with St.
Maria del Popolo in Rome as his titular church),
writes to the Duke as follows :—

"As I well know Your Excellency's inclination
for music and especially for that of Messer
Palestrina, I send you two (unspecified) of his
motets." This evidently led to a fresh commission, as Pierluigi writes, on December 15,
apologizing for the delay in sending certain
motets to words selected by the Duke. "I was
in bed," he says, "for many days, therefore they
will be feeble. Your Excellency must not be
surprised as they come from a convalescent."
This letter is of particular historical interest, for
Pierluigi refers to a custom in the Pope's Chapel,

and describes how the old *faux-boúrdon*, or simple
harmonization of the original plain-song usual in
the preceding century, had recently given place to
a free treatment, much the same as that Pierluigi
himself employed with such effect in the
Improperia. A description of this innovation may
help to make the point clear.*

"In the Sixtine Chapel the ritually-prescribed
Miserere was sung to a simple *faux-bourdon* chant.
The thrice-crowned friend of music" (Leo X.)
"seems to have wished for something more artistic
than this. . . ." And a little further on : "The
traditions of the earlier period of simple *faux-
bourdon* were still easily recognizable with their
four- and five-part strophes and the nine-part
closes." Obviously a choir of nine voices singing
antiphonally and joining for the closes. "In many
places the singers are only given the chord to
which they must themselves adjust the syllables
of the text to their proper declamatory accents ;
this is simple *faux-bourdon*. Other similar places
in which the harmony changes are naturally
written down. But between come flowing
polyphonic passages with distinct melodic themes,
with ingenious combinations of beautifully simple
imitations. The Epilogue unites both choirs in a
nine-part whole."

This description well explains the changes

* Ambros, *Geschichte der Musik.*

brought about by the development of polyphonic art. The old simplicity was not done away with, but served as the surface on which to embroider a new and beautiful pattern. The historical sequence was there, the antiphonal choir, one of the earliest embellishments of the primitive church-music ; the ancient melodies, first joined to rude harmonies, gradually enriched but always chiefly considered as a means of marking the proper declamatory accents ; now comes the beautiful efflorescence—the flowing passages with distinct melodic themes ; an art so admirably fitted for its purpose of accentuating and adorning the words it accompanies, that under favourable conditions the effect is stupendous.

To return to the letters : Pierluigi informs the Duke that as no copy exists of this new free species of *faux-bourdon* he has himself written it down for the use of the choir in St. Barbara, well knowing this would be pleasing to his patron.

The next letter in order is from Pierluigi again, and dated March 23, 1570, from which it is evident that the Duke has recently sent to Pierluigi a motet and madrigal for correction and criticism. Both are here given in a masterly compound of diplomacy and advice. In spite of the flattering terms employed he deals with the Duke faithfully, incidentally giving a little insight into his own methods of composition. " *Mi pare*," he says, " *ancora che per la stretta tessitura delle fughe, si occupino le parole alli ascoltanti.*" Or, " Also it seems to me that the close interweaving of the fugues will prevent the words from being audible to the listeners ; " and continues, " *ho segnati alcuni luoghi che mi par che quando si puo far di meno soni meglio l'Harmonia.*" Or " I have pointed out some places where it appears to me the effect would be improved by the reduction of parts." This letter was sealed with the device of a flowering plant, and scrollwise, Joannes. Petra. Loysio.

Five months later, on August 12, Don Annibale Capello writes to the Duke that he will shortly send him a motet by Pierluigi, composed for Philip II. of Spain. This is the one entitled *Domine in virtute tua*, included in the second volume of five-part motets published in 1572. Capello was the Duke's vassal and acted as his agent on many occasions, notably in matters concerning Church music. He was in the service of Cardinal d'Este, and dates this letter from Tivoli. The motet was duly sent to Duke William on September 2, with apologies for a poor copy, " as no one in Tivoli could be found to do it better." It may be mentioned here that the first book of motets, for five, six, and seven voices, published by Scoto, came out in 1569—the preceding year,

containing such gems as *O admirabile commercium :
O magnum mysterium ;* and the magnificent motet
for Ascensiontide, *Viri Galilaei ;* so that the
Duke's desire to possess new motets from Pierluigi's pen is comprehensible enough. Apart
from the historical interest of the letters, these
details serve incidentally to show the recognition
of Pierluigi's genius by his contemporaries and
the esteem in which his compositions were
held.

In 1572 the Duke came to Rome, and though
without a doubt Pierluigi was invited to his
presence the records are silent. The ensuing
letters show increased cordiality. In September
of that year Capello writes to the Duke that he is
sending him a book of motets for the use of the
choir of Santa Barbara, a new arrival from the
publishing house, Scoto of Venice. He adds,
Pierluigi thinks it unnecessary to write himself to
his patron as His Highness will be able to judge
from the dedication how much he—etc., etc.,—in
the usual flowery language of the time. Obviously
Capello was in Rome at that moment, in direct
communication with Pierluigi. The reception of
the motets evidently gratified the Duke. His
secretary, Zibramonte, also in Rome it appears, is
desired by letter to wait upon Pierluigi and make
him a present of twenty-five *scudi*, so " that he

* In present-day value about £35.

may see how much the Duke values the dedication." There was a fine flavour in the homage
certainly not lost on a connoisseur such as His
Highness of Mantua, for the volume contains
specimens as erudite as they are beautiful. The
motet *Tribularer si nescirem* may be compared to one
of those subtle locks of Florentine workmanship,
to the apparent simplicity of which years have
gone in the making. In it Pierluigi reiterates the
cry *Miserere mei Deus* at set intervals throughout
the whole composition, mounting, a step at a
time, to the fifth note of the mode, returning in
the same manner to the final. Only a contrapuntist will realize the quality of the achievement.
Again, in the motet, *Gaude Barbara beata*, in
honour of the Patroness of Duke William's
beloved church, there is perpetual imitation
between the various parts. It goes without saying that never once does scholarship here take
precedence of Pierluigi's habitual grace and
suavity. The good people of Mantua quite conceivably listened to the praises of Santa Barbara
on the day of her *festa*, totally unconscious of the
musical *tour de force* to which Messer Giovanni
Pierluigi treated them. But the Duke knew,
Giaches Wert knew, and, for the rest, the Court
of Mantua was a very home of learning, and
Pierluigi was sure of a discriminating appreciation
there if anywhere.

To the dedication on the first page of these motets a return must be made later, as it contains some highly interesting information, but for the moment it will be well to leave Mantua in order to consider certain changes which took place at this time in Pierluigi's fortunes.

CHAPTER VI

I T will doubtless not have been forgotten that
Pierluigi, on being dismissed from the
Pontifical Choir, was succeeded by Giovanni
Animuccia, who became likewise *Magister in musica
et cantû* to the Julian choir. This personage, a
Florentine of saintly life, an excellent musician,
was in close relation with his fellow-townsman,
the famous S. Filippo Neri,* one of the most
striking and lovable personalities of that period.
Among his many qualities S. Filippo was an
enthusiastic musician, and clear-sighted enough
to recognize music as a powerful auxiliary in
saving souls, certainly his predominant passion.
He thereupon founded an Order and included
among the rules drawn up for its discipline "the
contemplation of celestial things by means of
heavenly harmonies," a sixteenth-century equiva-
lent of "the education of the soul in virtue
by the movement of sounds." Carrying his

---

* Obviously "Saint" was a later addition, but it seemed natural
to speak of him by his better-known title.

conviction to a practical issue in a larger field, he inaugurated religious services non-liturgical in character about the year 1558, desiring thereby to attract those simple souls to whom St. Augustine's definition of hymns as " praise to God with song " could not fail to make its appeal.

At first these services took place in a small oratory from which his recently instituted Order took its name of Oratorians, but they won such an instant and overwhelming success that it became necessary to move, first to one, then to another church, as each in turn grew too small for the ever-increasing congregations, and finally Neri applied to the Pope for permission to build a church of his own, the still-existing *S. Maria in Vallicella*, popularly known as the *Chiesa Nuova*, or New Church. Long before this evidence of success S. Filippo enlisted the services of his friend Animuccia, who organized the music in conformity with the Saint's wishes. In conjunction with motets and litanies, *laudi*—hymns of praise originally chanted by Savonarola and his monks as they paced the streets of Florence seventy years earlier—were particularly in evidence. The words chosen were adapted to a well-known air in order that the people might sing them readily. Animuccia soon composed others in addition to these, sending them to the printing-press from whence they were issued—one volume in 1565,

another in 1570. Soon these congregational
services became known as " oratorios " from their
place of origin, the word acquiring later the
special significance in relation to musical form
which it has ever since retained. Music was thus
the bait by which S. Filippo lured souls to his
net, but he had still other means, labouring to
bring a love of Nature in its higher aspect into
the lives of men, thus directing them to the
Creator. To this end it was his custom to
conduct his flock to some hill on the confines of
Rome—a favourite spot being the grounds of the
present Villa Mattei on the Cœlian Hill—and
there engage in spiritual songs, merry conversation and the like, using the loveliness of the
scene before him to illustrate the love of God
towards mankind.

In 1571 his friend and coadjutor Animuccia
died. In the midst of his grief the Saint's
thoughts turned to Pierluigi, with whom it is not
unlikely he was already on friendly terms. Be
this as it may, he invited him to succeed the dead
musician as musical director of the oratorios, an
offer Pierluigi forthwith accepted, and applied
himself to the work with energy. There was
certainly a divine fitness in the choice, for whose
music could more effectually assist the congregation of the Oratorians, or the community itself, in
the contemplation of celestial things by means of

heavenly harmonies ?   A happier phrase than
that could not have been found to describe
Pierluigi's music.

But Animuccia's death had other conse-
quences. The post of Master of the Julian
Chapel was once again vacant. Possibly Pierluigi had never resigned himself to his dismissal
from the service of the Vatican, in spite of the
important posts he had meanwhile filled elsewhere.
At all events he left the service of the Cardinal
d'Este and applied for his old office.   It is
obvious that the Master of the Pope Marcellus
Mass was not likely to apply in vain, and he was
shortly back again in the position he filled on his
first brilliant promotion from the old cathedral
of S. Agapito.* The only difference was in the
title.   Formerly " Master of the Boys," his new
style was " Master of the Julian Chapel," with
four boys under his charge and a monthly salary
of six scudi and thirty-six bajocchi, instead of the
six scudi sixty bajocchi *and living expenses* he
received from the Cardinal, a sufficient answer to
the assertion made more than once recently that
Pierluigi showed a somewhat mercenary spirit.

According to the Abbé Baini, on taking up
his duties again at St. Peter's, Pierluigi lodged in
the choir-school attached to the Capella Giulia, a
building flanking the atrium of the old basilica

* April 1, 1571.

THE EASTER BLESSING GIVEN FROM THE BENEDICTION LOGGIA, ST. PETER'S. THE NEW BUILDING BEHIND.

From an anonymous 16th century engraving

not pulled down before 1605. Thanks to sketches preserved in the Vatican Library and elsewhere by M. v. Heemskerck, Grimaldi, and other anonymous artists, there is no difficulty in forming an idea of the precincts of old St. Peter's as they appeared in the middle of the sixteenth century. These show that the great piazza was far from presenting the appearance of to-day. The magnificent columns were not in place before 1667 : the fountains were erected still later : and the famous Egyptian obelisk brought to Rome by Caligula— the silent witness of so many bloody scenes of Christian martyrdom—stood at the side of the old basilica, where the sacristy now stands, to be moved only a few years later, by order of Sixtus V. in 1586,* to its present position, the centre of the great ellipse. In a drawing by Heemskerck, somewhat earlier in date, are shown the high walls enclosing the precincts of the Vatican, already some seven hundred years old, the Loggia, then unglazed, and with a free view on to the piazza, and the façade of the *atrium* forming a line with the so-called Benediction Loggia, from which, on the Thursday before Easter, the Bull " *In Coena Domini* " was publicly read. The whole of the space occupied at the present day by the façade alone was then filled by

---

* On which occasion Pierluigi's setting of the hymn *Vexilla Regis* was sung.

buildings, others flanked the *atrium* on the north side, serving various ecclesiastical purposes. In one of these, then, Baini asserts that Pierluigi was housed, under what conditions there is at present no evidence forthcoming. Here, on the very ground soaked by the blood of St. Peter, hallowed and sanctified to the faithful by every association, the Church's strong citadel, there were signs of great changes, the old order giving place to new. The ancient church was already half disintegrated, already the gigantic drum of the new dome, rising slightly to the left of the old building, commanded the entire precincts. In this unfinished state it remained for many years still, after the mighty brain which planned it was at rest, for means lacked (from Pius V.'s determination to put down the gross abuses connected with the sale of indulgences) to proceed with the erection of the new building. Another of Heemskerck's sketches,* taken from a point between the old and new churches, shows the ruined north transept, demolished to clear the way for the new construction, though a transverse wall screened it from the rest of the ancient basilica which continued for many years yet to fulfil its sacred functions. The demolition of this venerated building was certainly the most striking object on which the great musician's eyes rested,

* See p. 161.

while the erection of the new was a cause of never-failing interest.

From this great centre of the Church's life, Pierluigi continued to issue composition after composition. Taking into account his creative activity, as well as his ordinary professional work, it is obvious that his time was very fully occupied. But it is pleasant to hear that he yet found time to knit with S. Filippo Neri a close friendship destined to last as long as life itself. Of patrons we have heard in plenty, but this is the first friend of whom there is any record, and the personality of both saint and musician becomes more coherent through this simple fact. As Neri was much attached to Cardinal Carlo Borromeo it may be that Pierluigi found two friends instead of one, both men capable of sympathetic comprehension of his genius through their love of music. In the absence of any definite appreciation of Pierluigi as a man by his contemporaries this association acquires a particular value. If S. Filippo discovered in the musician qualities of mind and heart which won and retained his affection, it would be difficult to claim a finer testimony to the worth of Pierluigi's personality.

During these years two more volumes of motets appeared, also a new species of composition. The so-called *Madrigali Spirituali* (not published before

1581 and 1594 respectively) were written about this time for the members of S. Filippo's congregations. Simpler in form and composition than the style of music considered fitting for the Mass, they were thus well suited to the class to whom the Saint's services made their special appeal, and it may be assumed that they were often sung during those excursions to the hills of the *Gianicolo* and *Cœlio* of which S. Filippo was the organizer and leader. Here again was an instance of the changing times. To the almost pagan enjoyment of beauty and art and learning in which the Roman world was steeped when Pierluigi first entered it, a careful observance of religious ceremonies and duties was substituted. Though S. Filippo's teaching was on the same theme of beauty, he conceived it from the point of view of God's gift to man who, in his perception and use of it, must acknowledge this and render thanks to the Giver, worship and enjoyment becoming one. Pan and his pipes had again withdrawn to the ilex groves sheltering the ruined temples of a classic past, and the populace flocked around a new David with his harp. These spiritual songs on secular lines opened up fresh paths of spontaneity and expressiveness destined to bear fruit later on. But Pierluigi did not confine his pen to sacred madrigals, writing others secular, *pièces d'occasion* some of them, one

such being written to celebrate the victory of
Lepanto in 1571 :— *

    " Le selv' avea al lido Eusono
    Il superbe Ottoman col ferro tutte
    Recise "—

what time Don John of Austria and Marc
Antonio Colonna led the confederated troops
against the Turks. Such an occasion for a
madrigal from a loyal son of the Church requires
no excuse, but there was a diplomatic reason if
it were needed : Pierluigi and his family being
vassals of the Colonna and owning property in
their lordship.

A second volume of madrigals, though dated
1586, may be conveniently mentioned here, for
this was dedicated to Giulio Cesare Colonna, who
became Prince of Palestrina in 1571 † and died
in 1581, or five years before the date of publication of these madrigals ; thus giving rise to the
inference that it was a re-issue of an earlier edition
since lost, a theory strengthened by the innumer-
able misprints, for which only the circumstance of
a fresh edition, without the supervision of the
composer by Venetian publishers, would sufficiently account. This question of the date is
otherwise important. Two years before 1586, in

---

* The first book of madrigals appeared in 1555.

† A man of culture and learning and benefactor to his town,
so that Pierluigi had excellent reasons for desiring to dedicate his
madrigals to this Prince.

the dedication of the celebrated motets on the
Song of Solomon * to the reigning Pontiff,
Gregory XIII.,† Pierluigi beats his breast over
the sins of his youth, no other on this occasion
than the composition of madrigals ! It is somewhat difficult to take this *Apologia pro madrigali
sue* quite seriously, for he laments he is numbered
amongst those musicians who consecrated their
talents and their art to loves unworthy of the
name and profession of a Christian (!) the mild-
ness of the offence not justifying so tremendous a
self-condemnation. This raises the point referred
to earlier. If the second volume of madrigals
appeared first in 1586, what becomes of Pierluigi's
consistency ? Were they, however, written about
the time Giulio Cesare Colonna became reigning
Prince of Palestrina (in 1571) the difficulty dis-
appears, Pierluigi having ample time for repentance between these dates. Again, it was in
1571 that S. Filippo Neri invited him to replace
Animuccia as musical director of his services, a
time at which it may be supposed he fell under
the influence of the Saint, and his conscience
grew more sensitive. However this may be,
the manifestation of such austerity was nothing
unusual in these times. Such a spirit had always
existed, side by side with the looser ideas of the
Renaissance ; as, for instance, the assertion of

* Dealt with on pp. 131 *et seq.*   † Successor to Pius V.

Morales that he despised "all secular, let alone frivolous music : what should be said of such a one who prostituted the noble God-given gift to the service of frivolous worthless ends?" These words bear a strong resemblance to those used by Pierluigi in the dedication.

Amongst the madrigals in the above-mentioned volume is that entitled *Alle rive del Tebro*, perhaps the best known of all. Another, and one of the most beautiful, is *Amor quando floria :* the words of which are taken from Petrach's *ballata* in his *Death of Laura*, between the third and fourth cantos. In this form of composition Pierluigi was at his best when the words called for a gently elegiac setting, suited to the pure passionless sounds he of all musicians best understood. Our own countryman, Thomas Morley, puts the matter so well that we cannot do better than quote his words :—

"You must possesse yourselfe," he says, "with an amorus humour for in no cōposition shall you proue admirable except you put on and possesse yourself wholy with that vaine wherein you compose." For this reason, if that alone, Pierluigi was much more in his element when he proceeded to the composition of *madrigali spirituali*, which combined a beautiful idealism with a natural and human vein of expression. They may be described as the *canti popolari* of the

Church, and certainly served to spread his fame amongst that class of people to whom his masses and motets, for lack of musical knowledge, would make less appeal.

Pius V. died in May, 1572. He was buried in *S. Maria Maggiore*, where his tomb in the Sixtine Chapel is to be seen to-day. His whole strength was put forth in the cause of Church reform, and amongst his other activities connected with this end he was responsible for the revision of the breviary and missal, a logical outcome of the recommendations made by the Council of Trent during the preceding pontificate. Nor did he confine himself to the text alone. Once again there is an allusion to the burning question of eliminating all music other than the Gregorian chant from the Church in letters he wrote, in 1567, to the Bishop of Lucca, complaining of some musical performances during Holy Week in that town ; and again in 1570, over Church music in Mexico.* As all intercalations of text were now made illegal, the Master's mass *Ecce sacerdos magnus* was necessarily shelved ; another, *De beata Virgine*, was also affected ; but he was able to re-write the offending portions of this, and to issue a new edition.

About this time Pierluigi's financial circumstances again improved. According to a will

* Pastor, vol. viii.

dated November 7, 1572, his wife Lucrezia succeeded to the half of a small inheritance through the death of her sister Violante. Thus, taking into consideration the power of his patrons, the great activity of his pen, and his relatively assured position, it may be assumed that he was able to devote himself to his work without anxiety.

It is now time to ascertain what influence he exerted over contemporary musicians in Rome.

CHAPTER VII

THE prevailing tendency of musical art throughout the sixteenth century has already been grouped into two schools, each with a great name at its head, Josquin des Près and Giovanni Pierluigi da Palestrina. These may be said to have divided the century between them, for there was no outstanding composer between Josquin's death and Pierluigi's advent to weaken the earlier influence. There were also cross currents : sub-divisions, as it were, starting from the purely intellectual problems of the Netherlanders and tending towards the expressiveness and suavity of sound which gave the ultimate beauty and finish to the Roman School. The composers Morales and Festa may be placed in this category. Not until the last years of the century was there more than a hint of the new influences destined to sweep away that contrapuntal art so admirably adapted for the great basilicas and cathedrals. Thus Pierluigi had not to contend with alien influences and changing conceptions of artistic beauty, he maintained his prestige unimpaired until the end.

This being so, the number of his pupils, as far as is at present known, is surprisingly small. Though there are several who exhibit traits which stamp them as his spiritual children, only two outside his family circle can be named with certainty. These are Giovanni Andrea Dragoni, who claims Pierluigi as his master in the dedicatory address of a volume of his compositions; and Francesco Soriano, who is claimed by Pierluigi as his pupil in a letter written by him to William of Gonzaga, Duke of Mantua. The first-named pupil became choirmaster in the church of S. *Giovanni in Laterano* from 1581 until his death in 1594; the second, Soriano, became choirmaster in S. *Luigi dei Francesi* about 1581; after 1588 filling the same office in S. *Maria Maggiore*. At some time between these dates he was in the service of the Duke of Mantua to whom he dedicated a book of five-part madrigals. Born in 1549 he had, up till 1597, published only two volumes of madrigals, after which he turned to the composition of Church music. Pierluigi's appreciation of him as a musician will appear in a letter written to the Duke of Mantua later. Soriano composed music to the Passion of our Lord according to the four Gospels; showing a dramatic feeling for effect which gives him a place between the old and the new school.* He also

* Ambros, *Geschichte der Musik.*

composed a Hexachord mass described as one of
the most inspired works of the later Roman
School.*   No mere imitator of his master was
he, but a man full of energetic force of character.

But there is one who, never a pupil of Pierluigi's, produced compositions bearing the same
spiritual relationship to the master as if Pierluigi's
genius had found its feminine counterpart.   This
was Tommaso Lodivico da Vittoria, a Spaniard,
born at Avila about 1540.   He appears to have
been intended for the priesthood, and for that
reason was sent to the *Collegium Germanicum* in
Rome.   This celebrated College, founded by
S. Ignatius Loyola under Julius III. in 1552,
was considered as one of the most distinguished
places of education in Rome, nor was it created
solely for Teutons, but numbered amongst its
inmates members of noble families throughout
Europe.

The date on which Vittoria entered the
College was 1565, and by 1573 he was filling
the post of choirmaster there, receiving a commission to set to music the psalm, "By the
waters of Babylon," for a particular occasion, a
farewell service before the departure of the
students from their old home in the Palazzo
Colonna to their new one in the Palazzo della
Valle.   The College has had many flittings since

* Ambros, *Geschichte der Musik.*

then and its present home is in the Via San Nicolo
da Tolentino from whence its red-garbed students
continue to illuminate the streets of Rome, but,
in all that time, it has maintained its reputation for good music and possesses a list of
choirmasters of which any college might be proud,
including, as it does, such names as Giovannelli,
Pierluigi's successor at St. Peter's, Anerio,
Stabile, and the world-famous Carissimi. Vittoria
remained at the *Collegium Germanicum* until 1578,
after which date it is not yet established where he
lived and worked, though it has been suggested
that he followed Pierluigi as choirmaster of the
Altaemps Chapel.* However that may be, he is
reported to have been on the closest terms of
friendship with him. An anecdote exists that he
discarded his distinctive dress as a Spaniard for
one resembling that customarily worn by the
master, and trimmed his beard on the same
pattern. True or not, it is a pleasant story, and
must have had some foundation.

But if Vittoria copied Pierluigi's coat, his
genius remained independent. The most that
can be said is that the stronger fibre of his
great friend's mind influenced his own more
ardent, passionate, less robust temperament,

---

* The date of Pierluigi's activities at the Altaemps Chapel has
not yet been ascertained, only that he was director there for some
years.

which has been compared in certain aspects to that of Teresa of Avila, his compatriot, in its glowing mysticism. It is characteristic of the man that not a single secular composition of his has been found, in which respect he shows himself of one mind with his compatriot, Morales. While much of his work bears the true Palestrinian impress, yet Vittoria never quite reached those soaring, majestic heights to which Pierluigi rose at will. The Spaniard's note was more personal, more human, more pleading ; he gazed at the Cross as Mary Magdalene might have done.

It is said that through the jealousy of the Pontifical Choir, Vittoria was given no official post in the Vatican. If so, it was their loss. The state of his private circumstances is not known, but either he had a powerful patron, or was in possession of ample means, for he was able to bring out sumptuous editions of his works.

Other contemporaries were the two Naninos. The eldest brother, Giovanni Maria, a remarkable contrapuntist and one of the most learned musicians of his time, had a school of composition in which it has been suggested that Pierluigi taught. No confirmation of this can be found. Nanino's compositions warrant the inference that Pierluigi was his master ; for this reason he is sometimes spoken of as the founder of the Roman School, a statement manifestly absurd ; nevertheless, two of his compositions, *Hodie nobis coelorum est,* and *Hodie Christus natus est,* are frequently quoted as masterpieces imbued with true Palestrinian inspiration. Annibale Zoilo, Pierluigi's immediate successor at the Lateran, later, a member of the Pontifical Choir ; Felice Anerio, who began his career in 1575 as choir-boy under Pierluigi in the Julian Chapel and ended it in 1614 as Composer to the Pontifical Choir in Pierluigi's place (in 1585 choirmaster in the English College) ; Giovanelli, pure Palestrinian in style, Vittoria's successor at the *Collegium Germanicum* and Pierluigi's successor in the Julian Chapel,—all these were most excellent musicians and in high repute. Both Anerio and Giovanelli were particularly famous as madri-galists ; indeed, Anerio, until he entered upon his duties as Composer to the Pontifical Choir, was more known for this form of composition than for Church music. Ingegneri, a native of Verona born about 1545 (to 1550), whose life was chiefly spent in Cremona, and who composed Responses for Holy Week which for years were considered to be by Pierluigi—even appearing in the collected edition as *Opus dubium* until they were traced to their rightful owner ; Stabile, possibly a pupil of Pierluigi's ; and Allegri, a pupil of the elder Nanino, whose Miserere is still performed in Passion Week every year at

St. Peter's, were all educated in the true tradition
and carried on the glories of the school. Yet
others were Constantini, said to have represented
the " pure, noble style in its unadulterated form
long after the sun was setting on its dominion,"
and Vincenzo Ugolini, again a pupil of the elder
Nanino, and a typical member of the school.*

With one important exception † these, then,
are the names of the more outstanding members
of the Roman School. Pierluigi's figure domi-
nates them all; indeed, Vittoria, beautiful composer
as he was, moves in a subdued light in relation to
the great Palestrinian. This was clearly recognized,
even if the Netherlander Orlando di Lasso be
admitted as a formidable rival. But great as
Orlando was, there was a quality about Pierluigi's genius essentially individual and essentially
Roman. If the fancy be permitted, his style recalls the golden light of the Eternal City at
sundown, a distinctive glory which every one
familiar with it will at once recognize. This
is the more noteworthy as Music is the only
art Rome can claim as her own. Unrivalled as
she was in the attraction she exercised over the
great artists of all ages, she borrowed lustre from

---

* This is not intended as a comprehensive list. There were
many others, less celebrated, and men continued to compose in a
similar vein long after its prestige had been killed by the newer
methods.

† Marenzio,

their greatness, they were only her sons by
adoption.   In Pierluigi's case this was not so, and
obviously this fact was a source of peculiar satisfaction to the Romans, who may be said to have
smarted for upwards of three hundred years
under the foreign yoke of the Pontifical Choir.
The native musicians later took advantage of
their ascendancy to organize a society in which no
foreigners might be admitted, a sufficient indication of present strength and ancient jealousy,
though this rule was subsequently and wisely to
be relaxed.   Such close corporations have always
proved themselves against the best interests of the
art they were designed to help.

For the moment enough has been said to
justify the assertion that the Roman School was
an established fact, with Pierluigi as its chief
figure ; to sum up in the grandiose words of a
Venetian admirer,* writing some years later,
" he was the Ocean towards which all streams
flow."

* Giovanni Matteo Asola, 1592.

CHAPTER VIII

A T the end of the year 1572 death removed Pierluigi's great patron, Cardinal Ippolito d'Este. It is to be hoped that more will some day be known of their relations. The Cardinal's love for all forms of art was as much a mainspring in his life as his genius for diplomacy. The loss of so discriminating a patron was certainly a blow to the musician.

About the same time, however, an overwhelming personal sorrow befell Pierluigi. Of its nature we learn in a letter written by Bishop Odescalco to the Duke of Mantua, dated from Rome on January 3, 1573. This letter evidently refers to an earlier conversation between the Duke and Pierluigi, probably during the former's stay in Rome some months previously. Before giving the text we will return for a moment to the book of motets mentioned earlier as dedicated to the Duke, for the dedication throws some light upon the subject.*

In this the composer says :—

* See p. 78.

Quapropter haec tuo nomini consecro munuscula, in quibus interpositas quoque fratris, liberorumque meorum primitias non negliges deliberare, ut tibi non me unum duntaxat, veram etiam domum omnem meam plurimum debere non obscure cognoscas.

It thus appears that not only Pierluigi's two sons had profited by his teaching but his brother Silla also, all three adopting the profession of music. By offering these firstfruits from his sons' pen Pierluigi probably hoped to fulfil a double purpose ; not only to convince the Duke of his whole-hearted devotion, but also, with a father's far-seeing eye, to secure for his two boys the valuable patronage he himself enjoyed. Two motets were by his brother Silla, one each by his sons Ridolfo and Angelo. It is evident that Angelo possessed remarkable talent—he was only seventeen at the time,—while the work of his elder brother Ridolfo and his uncle Silla show a level of proficiency testifying to the soundness of their instruction if not suggesting so much force of inspiration. But it seems that Ridolfo's talents did not end here. As will presently appear, he was a proficient player on several instruments, giving colour to the supposition that Pierluigi directed and arranged chamber music for his patrons, an indispensable feature, at this time, of festive occasions. Hitherto Pierluigi's

inner life has remained more or less closed
to us. A temporary illness mentioned in the
letter to the Duke of Mantua, his friendship
with S. Filippo, his patrons, his surroundings—
so far as it was possible to reconstruct them—the
tradition of a happy marriage,—these were the
brief notes of a life which left itself more com-
pletely to be divined in the serenity and idealism
of his compositions. But now we get a singularly
attractive glimpse of a united family, two accom-
plished sons " of rare morals" of Pierluigi's
brother, and a devoted mother.

The Bishop writes :—

" The son promised to your Excellency by
Palestina (*sic*) for the service of S. Barbara died
a few days ago, and after him from sorrow, a
brother of Palestina himself, lettered, a good
musician by profession and of good morals. For
this reason it is useless to think more about it
and truly I hear from all that this young son of
Palestina was a young man who besides being
of suitable age, twenty-two years, was of very
good and rare morals, a good logician and
philosopher ; well educated in Greek and Latin,
and most excellent musician and player on all
sorts of instruments, so much so that I believe
he would have been after the heart of your
Excellency."

Here is a picture of the family of the great
musician which does him infinite credit. In the

midst of his own incessant work he yet saw to
it that his sons received the necessary education
for taking up a good position in life. " Most
excellent musician and player on all sorts of
instruments " might be expected, but " a good
logician and philsopher " suggests culture and
refinement beyond the ordinary. In the year
1566 both sons were entered as students in the
Seminarium Romanum, but appear later to have
abandoned the intention of becoming priests.
The Bishop continues—

" There remains still another son of eighteen
to nineteen, who has almost all the same good
qualities, but I hear his mother will never consent
to be deprived of him, having lost that one of
so much promise as well as his uncle in twenty
days."

Of Ridolfo the eldest son, there was already
a glimpse in earlier days, as choir-boy in the church
of *S. Giovanni in Laterano.* That was twelve
years ago ; now it was a question of establishing
him in life, and his father hoped to place him in
the brilliant court of Mantua for the service of
which he had so well prepared him. Pierluigi's
brother, Silla, is a more shadowy figure, " lettered,
a good musician by profession and of good
morals." It remains still to be discovered if he
held any important post in one of the Roman
churches, or whether he devoted himself to his

celebrated brother, helping him in his professional
work.

This double bereavement marks a turning-
point in Pierluigi's career, and from henceforth
sorrow dogged his footsteps. Soon come many
references to ill-health and misfortune. But he
never faltered in his work and it may very well
be that composition was the staff on which he
leant in those dark days, and which brought him
comfort. On April 17, 1574, the veil is again
lifted for a moment when Annibale Capello writes
to the Duke that Pierluigi is too busy to criticize
a mass written by his great patron in Mantua,
whose ambition has evidently been spurred on
by praise. In Capello's courtier-like phrases the
almost startling truth emerges that Pierluigi is
engaged on work of even more importance than
that most important mass which reveals the
Duke as much " master of the Muses as of the
Mantuans ! "—a neat compliment which it is to
be hoped the Muses, who are more used to be
wooed than governed, did not resent. The
momentous work on which Pierluigi was engaged
was a new set of Lamentations commissioned by
the Pope himself (Gregory XIII.). In Capello's
words :—

"Et a credere insieme che l'occupationi di
M. Gio da Palestina (*sic*) in comporre alcune
lamentationi per ordine del Papa e nella cappella

di questi giorni santi hanno fatto tardare esso
M. Gio a fare alcune poche considerationi et
auertimenti sopra la detta compositioni : le quali
si conosce bene essere stati da lui pretermessi per
hauer atteso a cose maggiori."

Which may be translated :—

"And likewise to believe that M. Gio da
Palestina's labours in composing some lamentations by the Pope's orders and in the choir
during these holy days have caused M. Gio to be
behindhand in making some few remarks and
observations on the said composition, which we
can well understand have been pretermitted by
him because he had to attend to greater matters."

This letter, not hitherto mentioned in
existing biographies, refers to a set of Lamentations which it may be well here to point out were
anterior to those composed some years later for
Sixtus V., not those, in short, which that Pope
insisted (to the discomfiture of the Pontifical
Choir) upon substituting for some hitherto in use
by Carpentras. Pierluigi wrote four sets in all,
the last being the first set to be published.* The
Lamentations referred to by Capello were either
those found in the Altaemps Chapel, or still
another set supposed by Haberl to have been
written while Pierluigi was Master of the Choir
at *S. Maria Maggiore.* The evidence is in

* It is to be found in vol. xxv. of the complete edition.

favour of the latter hypothesis, as there exists in the library of the Cappella Julia a beautiful codex, on the first page of which is written in Pierluigi's handwriting :—

" libro contenente le lamentationi della settimana santa del Palestrina ; "

identified as that attributed to the S. Maria Maggiore period. The point is of importance, as the first three sets bear neither date nor dedication.

On the same date as that on which Capello's letter was written Pierluigi himself wrote to the Duke, apologizing for his delay and making a few rather perfunctory criticisms, though they were set forth with the usual complimentary additions. Ten months later, on February 9, 1575, he writes again, addressing the Duke by his recently acquired title—" Duke of Mantua and Montferrata," bestowed by the Emperor Maximilian II., and it is evident, from the nature of the letter, that he has been commissioned by his patron to set a *canzone* to music, though this has not yet been identified. One more incident in this year : the Chapter of S. Maria Maggiore tried to tempt Pierluigi to return to them by the time-honoured expedient of offering him a larger salary. Pierluigi took the favourable opportunity of convincing the Chapter of St. Peter that they had necessarily no monopoly of his services, and the Chapter recognized the cogency of the argument by raising his very moderate stipend to fifteen scudi, " in consideration of the worth and excellence of his person," thus honouring themselves in their appreciation of their *Magister Capellae Juliae.* The matter was settled by the employment of white and black beans ; those in favour of the proposition using white, those against, black. A single black bean was discovered in the urn. It would be interesting to know who was the Beckmesser !

This pleasant little episode was hardly needed to show that Pierluigi was now receiving full public recognition. It was not to be expected that this should yet be complete—a man's reputation rarely attains to this in his lifetime, and when it does it is not infrequently an unhealthy sign for its duration. But in the same year and in the last place where a prophet's fame is supposed to establish itself—in his own country —Pierluigi's fellow-citizens gave a signal proof of their pride and joy in their great townsman.

It was the year of the Jubilee, and a great procession of some fifteen thousand persons streamed through the ancient gate of Palestrina on their way to Rome. The banners of the Confraternities of the Crucifixion led the way, followed by the Blessed Sacrament. The

Palestrinians formed themselves into three choirs, and entered Rome singing Pierluigi's music. What they sang has not been recorded, only that it was " tre belle musiche," a statement easy of acceptance. This beautiful homage and public recognition from their own people was certainly very gratifying to Pierluigi and his wife Lucrezia, and the memory would long abide with them.

But joy was short-lived. Another great sorrow befell them, and their son Angelo died ; at a moment when life must have presented its most desirable aspect. Married while extremely young—he cannot have been more than nineteen at the time—he chose a wife from his father's birthplace, a rich burgher's daughter who brought him as dowry some 1740 scudi.* In February, 1574, the young couple hired a house in the *Borgo* (as the district within the fortified Leonine City was called) in the *Piazza delli Scarpellini*, and there their first child was born who was baptized in November of that year. In 1576 a son, Angelo (the first was a daughter, Aurelia) followed, the year of his father's death. There is nothing to show what struck the young man

This, according to custom, was secured on her father-in-law's property, and we incidentally learn that Pierluigi possessed one house in the *contrada Egypti*, another in the *regione Parionis in contrada Sarti*, and a vineyard near the ancient and beautiful church of S. Lorenzo outside the walls.

down, but this new blow fell only three years after the death of Ridolfo, so it is no matter for astonishment that Pierluigi's health was shaken. Even the most buoyant nature could scarcely hope to react from so much grief, and in Angelo it is probable Pierluigi's hopes of a successor were centred, for the motet which is all that is at present known of his compositions much surpasses that of his brother or uncle. Though Ridolfo and Angelo were the only sons mentioned in the Bishop's letter : there was still a younger one, by name Igino. Of his personality the accounts are somewhat conflicting, but on the whole are not in his favour. Of him more later. There is no doubt that in Ridolfo and his brother Angelo Pierluigi possessed sons who would have brought great credit to their father's name, and with them disappeared much of the happiness life could afford him.

We now come to a transaction which is far from clear. On October 25, in that year (1576), the Pope issued a brief that the *Directorium Chori* was to be revised. This was an inevitable sequence to the revision of the Breviary and Missal already completed in the previous reign. Obviously a colossal undertaking, it demanded unremitting attention and a corresponding expenditure of time. As was only to be expected, Pierluigi, with Annibale Zoilo, his successor at

S. Giovanni in Laterano, was requested to do the work. It is said that the *Graduale* was actually completed, Pierluigi undertaking the *Temporale* and Zoilo the *Sanctorale* as their respective shares, when, for some unknown reason, they abandoned the project and made no attempt to get their already completed work published. Why? There are various conjectures but no certainty. One explanation was that the revisers treated the ancient chant too drastically ; making alterations in the melodies and thus incurring the wrath of conservative persons. In support of this theory it remains on record that a certain Fernando de Las Infantas complained to no less a person than Philip II. of Spain on the subject, gaining his approval and valuable support in subsequent representations to the Holy Father. Another suggestion is that Pierluigi and Zoilo found they were expected to do the work for fame alone and, not being content with this, left it uncompleted. Were it so, that were as good a reason as any other : the labourer, indeed, being worthy of his hire ; but that would have constituted a grievance, and there is no reason to suppose that Pierluigi considered himself badly treated. In 1582 the Bolognese, Giovanni Guidetti, one of Pierluigi's reputed pupils, also Chaplain to Gregory XIII., brought out his revision of the *Directorium Chori,* with a laudatory preface by Pierluigi. Surely this disposes effectually of the supposition that there was anything unpleasant in the affair? Guidetti followed this publication up with a setting of the Passion according to each of the four Gospels, an Office for Holy Week, the Lamentations, and the Prefaces. All these without any protest whatever from either Pierluigi or Zoilo; indeed, in one instance, Pierluigi's co-operation is actually suspected. As far as posterity is concerned, it is evident that Pierluigi was more advantageously employed in giving to the world his masses and motets than on work which any good musician with the historical sense, with judgment and accuracy, could do as well; and it is not impossible that, perceiving this himself, he nominated Guidetti as a substitute. Yet one other possible explanation, a reference to which occurs in a letter from Annibale Capello to the Duke of Mantua under the date October 18, 1573, may be advanced here. He tells the Duke that Pierluigi has been unable to give effect to certain wishes expressed by his patron on account of grave indisposition affecting both his head and his sight. Here is sufficient reason for abandoning a task involving great strain on eyesight, as well as close application. A letter from Pierluigi himself, a fortnight later, refers to his illness and in the following terms :—

I

"God knows that when the *canti fermi** were brought to me 1 was more distressed at my inability to serve you than by my illness."

In a preceding letter Capello had written on a subject very near to the Duke's heart, the purity of the plainsong, and Pierluigi in his reply proceeds to give interesting details upon the disposition of the voices in a mass he had recently composed, the wording of the whole permitting the inference that the Duke had given him a similar commission to the one he was at that time engaged on for the Pope, the revision of the Ecclesiastical Chant.   Here is the passage—

"Et se l'Altezza V si contentara si mandaranno in stampa con il graduale che nostro signor mi ha commandato ch'io emendi."

That is—

"If Your Highness agrees, these chants can be printed with the Gradual with whose revision His Holiness has commissioned me."

As in the next letter a princely gift from the Duke of one hundred scudi † is mentioned, it may be assumed that Pierluigi had completed the work and satisfied his patron. During the rest of that year he continued to be deeply engaged

* The Duke evidently selected the melodies himself on which he wished certain compositions to be constructed.
† About £125 in present-day value.

in his service, for he himself mentions three masses undertaken at the Duke's request, and Capello refers to others.

From 1580 to 1583 there is a gap in the letters and it is necessary to turn to other sources of information for particulars of Pierluigi's life during these years. Through the Register of Deaths belonging to St. Peter's, we learn that Lucrezia, Pierluigi's wife, after a married life lasting thirty-three years, died and was buried on July 23, 1580, in the *Cappella Nuova* of St. Peter's. The mother did not therefore long survive the death of her sons. Pierluigi, however, does not appear to have been left entirely alone. His youngest son, Igino, married Virginia Guarnacci in 1577, and in the register of St. Peter's occurs an entry referring to the baptism of their son Tommaso whose godfather was no less a person than Cardinal Sirleto. This member of the Sacred College occupied himself keenly in questions affecting the conservation of the ancient chant in its purity,* which may be taken as a sufficient explanation for his patronage of Pierluigi and his family. But it is to be surmised that the domestic situation was no easy one. Pierluigi had not only lost his beloved wife but the head of his household. As Master of the

---

* It will be recalled that Sirleto wrote to Cardinal Cervini before he became Marcellus II., on this subject.

Julian Choir he had boys under his care, and a young daughter-in-law with small children—a baby was born only three days after Lucrezia's death—may quite conceivably have lacked the experience and leisure for the management of so complicated a household. Be this as it may, in 1581, Pierluigi married again, choosing a wife suitable to a man of advancing years and failing health. Victoria Dormuli was a rich widow and beyond this little is known of her, the only documents throwing any light on the subject dealing with the business transactions incidental to a prosperous fur business she inherited from her first husband. From this she chiefly, though not entirely, derived her income, and according to a document discovered in recent years, Pierluigi figured in it as her partner until the business was placed in other hands for management. As nothing was known of this second marriage until the end of the nineteenth century, the Abbé Baini, relying on the circumstance that Pierluigi's first marriage was known to be a very happy one, built up a romantic story of his despair, proceeding to give pathetic details of compositions produced under its influence. Obviously Pierluigi's speedy remarriage does not in any way exclude the genuineness of his profound sorrow. No one has the right to gauge the quality of such a grief on grounds like these. All honour to Victoria

Dormuli, who was ready to aid the great musician at so sad a crisis in his history. And before the year was out Death robbed him of his little grandchildren, Angelo's son and daughter, who were left to their grandfather's charge on the remarriage of their young mother. Is there any cause for astonishment that Pierluigi sought to make headway against his misfortunes by building up his life again, or had felt the need of assistance in protecting the two young children in his care?

CHAPTER IX

IN the year 1581 a new name appears in the annals of Pierluigi's life, that of a man to whose splendid and attractive figure it would not be difficult to write dedicatory epistles *con amore*. This was the young Duke of Sora, a son born to Gregory XIII. before he entered the priesthood. Tiepolo, the Venetian ambassador at the Papal Court, in a confidential report to his Government, describes him as well-versed in letters, graceful in manners, of a noble and liberal mind, with ability and judgment for anything to which he might apply his powers. In the Colonna Palace, hard by the church of the *Santi Apostoli*, he and his wife—a daughter of the House of Sforza—lived magnificently ; and his entertainments were estimated as among the most brilliant Rome afforded, no light estimation in those days of gorgeous hospitality. The guess may be hazarded that Pierluigi had the direction of the inevitable music at these, for, in a dedication, he speaks of favours received from the Duke who, as was to be expected, would hardly fail to enlist the services of the foremost musician at the Papal Court in organizing those noble fêtes. The Palazzo Colonna was in itself a miniature Court, frequented by all who wished to be in the favour of the Pontiff, and if—as is probable—the Duke shared his father's marked predilection for the society of musicians (a predilection which was actually made a subject of reproach to the Pope in the last years of his Pontificate), the connection may be regarded as not only profitable but adding largely to the amenities of Pierluigi's life. Be this as it may, he dedicated to his young patron a book of motets for four voices, and the first book of *madrigali spirituali* already mentioned as written for the use of S. Filippo's congregations.

In the following year a fresh volume of masses appeared, dedicated to His Holiness. Of these, four out of seven were copied into the choir-books of the Sistine Chapel under distinctive titles, Pierluigi previously having designated them only by numbers. *Missa Prima* thus became *Lauda Sion; Missa Tertia, Jesu nostra redemptio;* while a second *Missa Tertia* for five voices—the preceding were for four—received the title *O magnum mysterium.* This mass was already written in 1571, the year of Pierluigi's return to St. Peter's, as is shown by the date worked into the ornamental design of the Q in *Qui tollis. Missa Prima* has as its basic theme a melody proper to the

Feast of *Corpus Christi ; Missa Tertia,* for four voices, the hymn for Ascensiontide, *Jesu nostra redemptio ;* while *Missa Tertia* for five voices is taken from Pierluigi's motet *O magnum mysterium.* "Why," it may be asked, "was it necessary to disguise these masses under a numerical nomenclature if, as appears, the origin of their themes was in conformity with the injunctions of the Council of Trent ? " There *is* a reason though one only recently discovered. *Missa Quarta* conceals an old friend under its non-committal title. It is the second of Pierluigi's masses written on the famous melody " L'homme armé," again a proof that Pierluigi saw no harm in the practice of using secular themes as long as they were so employed that the mere layman had no opportunity of being scandalized thereby.

It is curious to learn, at this time, that notwithstanding his favourable circumstances in Rome, Pierluigi evidently contemplated going to live in Mantua under the Duke's protection. It may be that he was grown restless under the savage blows Fate had dealt him, * and desired to seek fresh scenes, unhaunted by sad memories. At first there is no direct reference to the affair, but it may be inferred, after some preliminaries of which there is no record, that the Duke sent his

---

* Indeed, within only a few months he had lost another grandchild, Igino's little son,

secretary, Aurelio Zibramonte, to sound Pierluigi on the subject. If so, it was approached in what may be termed the diplomatic manner, for Zibramonte asks Pierluigi to give his opinion on the merits of other musicians, subsequently writing to the Duke as follows :—

"Messer Giovanni da Palestrina discussed with me the project of making Messer Annibale Zoilo your choirmaster and will find out his point of view, and Don Annibale Capello tells me that Palestrina would be ready to serve your Highness, also commending his son who is a good musician, but I do not know the conditions to which he pretends."

This letter, dated March 26, 1583, was followed by another a fortnight later :—

"Palestrina finds that Zoilo will not leave [Rome] on account of his wife and children and therefore falls back on Messer Luca Marentio, who serves the Cardinal d'Este, and S.S.S. thought of sending him to the King of France, for which reason he would not concede him to the Duke of Ferrara his brother."

Here are highly interesting references to matters which require more explanation than they receive in the letter. Luca Marenzio—so his name is usually spelt—was not mentioned amongst Pierluigi's contemporaries in the short account given of these, for he cannot altogether be considered a typical member of the Roman School, but rather as a genius trained in it and finding his own brilliant path later. He takes rank as one of the most important musicians towards the latter decades of the century. Born in the neighbourhood of Brescia about 1550 he was thus a man of thirty-three at this time. As a writer of Church music his motets *O quam gloriosum* and *Hodie Paulus Apostolus* are particularly fine examples of a style based on the Palestrinian School ; but as a writer of madrigals he stands so high as to need a niche for himself. In this form of composition he uses chromatic harmonies previously unknown, and though a great quantity of his works have not yet been translated into modern notation, sufficient is in existence to convince the student that Marenzio was little short of three hundred years in advance of his time. This is not, however, the place for the study of so interesting a personality. His reputation at the moment in which Zibramonte wrote to the Duke was already so high that he might well be considered a dangerous rival to Pierluigi himself " who," the letter continues, " affirms that this Marentio is not a better man than Soriano," Pierluigi's pupil, " neither in science, nor as a director of music (*in attitudine di gouernar musici*), and therefore counsels your Highness to think of some one else." There is no reason to suspect Pierluigi of insincerity here, nor of undue preference for his pupil, Soriano, who, as has already been pointed out, was a remarkable musician. Marenzio's madrigals were not here in question and as a writer of Church music, his work might fairly be compared with that of other excellent composers of that school, of whom Soriano was a typical example. It seems highly probable that Pierluigi was out of sympathy with Marenzio's secular compositions which, it is even reasonable to suppose, may have struck him as fantastic, revolutionary, almost unintelligible. Verily the old order changeth, giving place to new, and those of the old order often suffer from an inability to grasp the significance of experiments outside their own artistic experience. So much, then, for Marenzio, though the subject is tempting enough. But there remains another reference to a matter of historical interest which affords another instance of the high estimation in which music and musicians were at this time held. The Cardinal d'Este mentioned by Zibramonte was not, of course, Pierluigi's former patron, who had been dead for some years, but a son of Duke Ercole II., brother of the reigning Duke, Alfonso II. This Cardinal, Luigi d'Este, filled the ecclesiastical office of Protector of France, for which reason he was styled *Sua Santa Signoria*,—abbreviated as the S.S.S. of the letter. This sufficiently explains why he

desired to perform the pleasing service of sending
His Majesty the King of France such a distinguished musician as Marenzio.

Pierluigi's pupil Soriano was, at this moment,
in the Duke of Mantua's service, but it appears to
have been in the nature of a temporary appointment which might become permanent ; some such
inference may be drawn from Zibramonte's next
letter, dated four days later :—

" Messer Giovanni da Palestrina has been to
tell me this morning that for the love he bears his
pupil Soriano it would displease him if he lost his
position in your Highness's service on his account,
but being devoted, as he is, to your Highness,
does not wish to fail in holding himself ready to
serve you, together with his young son aged
twenty-two, who has a wife and a little son, and
is studying the law, hoping to take his degree as
Doctor in a year, after which your Highness will
be able to employ him in your service as you may
think suitable.   I tried to find out what salary he
desired, but always with much modesty he replied
that he would serve your Highness for nothing if
his circumstances permitted.   He would be satisfied with what was seemly and desired as much as
would provide for himself and his family so that
he was relieved from care on their account.   Here
he has 200 ducats (each of the value of 10 Julii)
from the Chapter of St. Peter's for life as long as
he serves them.   He has a letter from His Holiness on this point according to which he cannot

be deprived of this sum during his service. This proceeding has displeased the Chapter and interferes with the privilege of His Holiness to dismiss him at their pleasure.* Besides this, from other sources of income and from casual fees he receives about 50 ducats. He has also a certain income from His Holiness that he hopes will not be taken away from him if he enters your Highness's service. His family numbers seven mouths, namely himself, his wife, his son, his daughter-in-law, the little grandchild, a man-servant, a maid. He wishes your Highness to pay the cost of the journey to Mantua and to house them in such a manner that they may live comfortably."

This highly important letter gives the first opportunity of making an authoritative statement of Pierluigi's income at this time, and its discovery was the first indication of the hitherto unknown fact of his remarriage. Though the value of money constantly changed according to its purchasing power in the sixteenth century, the sum of two hundred ducats which formed Pierluigi's salary from the Chapter of St. Peter's may be reckoned as equal to fifty pounds, at present-day value two hundred and fifty pounds. About a quarter of that sum may be added to it from uncertain sources. The amount of the pension from the Pope's private purse is not specified. These

---

* Apparently the Chapter were annoyed that the Pope had bound himself to retain Pierluigi's services independently of their will.

amounts, which are reckoned at the rate of a little over five times and a half as much, or rather under than over the estimated value according to modern computations, were the reward of his labours in connection with St. Peter's and do not include such items as fees for dedications to patrons, or for professional work elsewhere, for instance, in the Altaemps Chapel, etc., for it can hardly be supposed that these went unremunerated. Nor is there any mention here of income invested in private property, which would naturally remain outside the present discussion. The reference to his son, Igino, in the letter throws much light on that young man's history. There is no allusion elsewhere to his professional calling, though Zibramonte's first letter states he is a good musician. Evidently Pierluigi regarded this as sufficiently important to be worthy of mention. He foresaw for his son a sphere of usefulness in a double capacity at the Mantuan Court. Now that Igino's profession is revealed it goes far to explain the love of litigation characteristic in later days, as well as a certain tendency to sharp practice which, however, defeated its own ends. Once again this letter illustrates Pierluigi's admirable care for his family, his desire to include them in any good fortune he might enjoy. There can be little doubt that this wrecked the project. " Provision for seven mouths," that illuminating phrase, was

a heavy addition to the Duke's budget, and
William of Mantua was, although a generous
patron, a prudent man. In spite of his appreciation and admiration of the great musician, his
earnest desire to give to Mantua the best the
times afforded, he was careful not to imperil his
engagements towards others already in his service
by a too lavish expenditure on a new undertaking.
So much is shown by the letters during the
months of April and May, for those written on
behalf of the Duke, while displaying eagerness, ask
for a more explicit statement of Pierluigi's wishes
regarding salary and expenses, desiring to know
whether he is strong enough to bear the strain of
Court life, the constant journeys in the Duke's
train, the consequent separation from wife and
family. To those acquainted with the chronicles
of Court festivities in Milan and Ferrara—to
mention only two of the numerous Courts
throughout Italy celebrated for the splendour of
their entertainments—these inquiries will seem
pertinent enough. They may even have suggested doubts to Pierluigi himself, at this moment
not far removed from sixty and in failing health.
The Bishop of Alva, who now acts as go-between,
is requested by the Duke to confine the bargain
within certain financial limits and to inform Pierluigi that his Highness possesses a house in
Mantua where he and his family may live in

comfort ; further, that the expenses of the journey will be borne by the Duke. In another letter, from the Duke's secretary, Giaches Wert's name is mentioned, and we learn that he is content with a salary of one hundred *scudi*, a house, and provision for two mouths ; still, it is evident his Highness is very anxious to persuade Pierluigi, for after a night's reflection, he follows up this letter with another desiring the good Bishop to tell Pierluigi he will undertake to employ the son who is about to receive his doctor's degree, and that his Highness's service, always lucrative, will be made doubly so to one coming from Rome, and thoroughly conversant with ecclesiastical procedure. But the Bishop writes that he has not succeeded in getting a definite statement from Pierluigi, though he hears from a third person, Annibale Capello, that the great musician will not leave Rome without a yearly stipend of two hundred ducats, the sum he already receives from the Chapter of St. Peter, not forgetting the provision for seven mouths. This constitutes a deadlock. The correspondence here breaks off and the rest is silence. Whether the Duke desired Annibale Capello to tell Pierluigi that his terms were too high, whether a letter from Pierluigi, withdrawing from the transaction, is lost, the net result was that he remained in Rome. Possibly other considerations had their weight.

Rooted deep in the life of the Papal Court, Pierluigi was no longer young, Mantua was far from
Rome and friends, far, too, from his property
both here and in Palestrina ; his heart may very
well have failed him before the final step. In any
case, from whichever side the decision came the
negotiations left no bitterness behind. The correspondence proceeds on the old lines of mutual
respect and appreciation. After all, who could
regret that Pierluigi remained in Rome, the faithful
servant of St. Peter's, head of that grand school
of composition recognized and admired by all ?
Something in weight and dignity he would
assuredly have lost as the Duke's choirmaster,
even were the material advantages greater. Rome
moulded him, crowned him, if sometimes the
crown was of thorns, and the time was coming
when her sacred dust would mingle with his, the
imperishable part of him remaining to pulsate
through the mighty church and to the summit
of the great dome that her musician did not
live to see completed. Considerations such as
these may very well have stood for something in
the abandonment of a plan, it may be, born of
restlessness, the outcome of his sorrows, of the
daily frictions and annoyances which attend the
life of every great artist.

K

CHAPTER X

BETWEEN the years 1582 and 1584 details are again lacking of Pierluigi's life. But in 1583 there is just one glimpse of him, for the Company of Rome—so it was styled—came into existence, a society created, it appears from the evidence, to assist that scheme, dear to the heart of every Roman, of ousting the foreigner. In this object it obviously co-operated with the Julian Choir, partly founded for a similar purpose. This conclusion is based on two facts : that the Pontifical Choir, composed largely of foreigners, fought it tooth and nail, passing a resolution condemning any of its members to a fine who had dealings with the Company of Rome, and that the list of the Company consisted exclusively of native musicians.* On this ground an explanation of the circumstance that Vittoria the Spaniard was not made a member may be sought. The quarrel between the Pontifical Choir and the Company of Rome did not endure,

* Thus were the foundations laid of a national school which, in a reorganized form, exists to-day as the Academy of St. Cecilia.

for already in 1589 a collection of madrigals
issued by the latter and edited by Anerio, there
described as Master of the Choir, included
amongst the compositions of Pelestino (*sic*) Dragoni, Soriano, Marenzio, Stabile, Giovanelli, Bernardino Nanino and others, works by three
members of the Pontifical Choir. The publication, by the way, was quaintly entitled *le gioie*, or
the jewels.

From 1584 onwards the thread may be picked
up once more as there are two letters from Pierluigi to the Duke of Mantua, the first of which,
dated August 27, begins : " The boundless
obligations I have towards your Highness," and
proceeds to offer him a copy of the " new book of
motets on the Song of Solomon." These magnificent compositions had a complete and instant
success. Baini surpasses himself in their pane-
gyric and with reason, for the Master is here a
creator of a new species of composition. It must
always be borne in mind that if a modern composer wishes to set this or that text to music he
has an inexhaustible fount of musical types to
choose from, proceeding to adorn it by the light
of any originality in himself. He may, indeed,
accomplish his task in a form having all the appearance of a new idiom ; it will not be long, however,
before the critics have discovered this or that
analogy ; this or that derivation from other

composers ; or, failing that, the use of some ancient
theory of sound or scale. In the sixteenth century
it was otherwise. Composers, then, were not
compelled to choose between a more or less
marked plagiarism or eccentricity. They were
groping their way step by step along a beautiful
strange road ; led spiritually, with the better
expression of the Church's meaning as their
guiding star. In the preface Pierluigi speaks of
genere alacriore—of a more animated species.
There was already a breath of this spirit in the
madrigali spirituali, hardly ecclesiastical, certainly
not secular ; rather—warm, human, expressive.
But here he is aided by the quality of the text
and the marvellous imagery of the Eastern King's
poem, liberating a quality of expressiveness which
the reticence of the Church musician had previously held in reserve. There must be no
misunderstanding here. There was no attempt
at realism, for the Bible was still the Sacred Book,
not having yet become the gold-mine for the
scene-painter, the playwright, the musician. To-
day, danced to a chromatic tone-scheme which has
little or nothing in common with the music of the
East, the story of the Baptist and the daughter of
Herodias furnishes a stage-setting for the newest
dancer or for the display of the latest harmonic
effect. Joseph provides a study of erotic emotion ;
Samson the spectacle of the strong man entangled

in the siren's toils. Already Solomon's beautiful
poem is transferred to the film of a cinematograph,
possibly with music illustrative of "The beloved
skipping upon the hills," or "The little foxes
spoiling the grapes." Without dwelling further
on the consequent loss and degradation, Pierluigi's
music may be recommended to those who grieve
at such a state of things. In these exquisite
motets, written before the operatic idea had taken
root in human consciousness, is to be found the
one tolerable medium for conveying a passionate
symbolism that only man in the beauty of a
pastoral simplicity might dare to use. Not a
vestige of the dramatic or the sensuous is *there*, but
a longing so etherealized, so rare that it forms a
truly wonderful expression of soaring idealism.
The music interprets an inner ecstasy not to be
reached through the medium of words. Here is
something more than the old Platonic definition
of the movement of sounds so as to reach the
soul for the education of it in virtue; much
more than the Renaissance ideal of pure beauty,
for it adorns these conceptions with spirituality.

In the letter accompanying the gift of this
volume to the Duke Pierluigi communicates the
fact that he has another work in hand. This was
probably his fifth book of motets, published in
that year by Gardano of Rome, and dedicated to
the young Cardinal-prince, Andrea Bathory,

nephew of the famous and knightly Stephen, King of Poland. This young man, of extremely pious disposition, was sent by his uncle on an embassy to the Papacy late in 1583. Delighting in music, he naturally sought out Pierluigi, who was at that moment in full enjoyment of the fame and acclamation his motets on the Song of Solomon brought him. Delighted with the pleasant, graceful manners of the young prince, Pierluigi forthwith desired to pay him the compliment of a dedication before his departure from Rome, and hurried this fifth book of motets through the press, adding compositions not originally intended in the scheme. Thus *Surge Sancte Dei de habitatione tua* and *Ambula Sancte Dei ad locum predestinatum* are motets belonging to the year 1580 ; written for certain solemn festivities which took place in connection with the transference of the relics of St. Gregory Nazianzen. While Bathory was in Rome Gregory presented him with the Cardinal's hat, for which reason his stay was prolonged beyond his original intention, and Pierluigi therefore had the pleasure of presenting the new volume in person. It was a high compliment to pay, for among the contents of this book, surely worthy of the title given by the Company of Rome to their firstfruits, are to be found such "jewels" as the motet for Ascensiontide, *Tempus est ut revertar* and the exquisite *Salve*

Regina. The flummery of the dedication reads in sharp contrast with the high morality of these noble works, but these things must be accepted with philosophy. Disparities in station and rank yawned wider then than now; though kings might, and did, pick up the paint brushes of geniuses, though an amazing liberty of speech was permitted between Pope and craftsman, though poetasters and dramatists enjoyed nothing less than public adulation, the barrier was insurmountable and all were at the mercy of a more or less arbitrary will. There were always bold spirits whom not even a dungeon could subdue; still, for the most part, the artist, intent on securing a quiet and safe life for the prosecution of his studies, surrounded himself with patrons as great and as powerful as circumstances permitted, and addressed them in language as obsequious as their ratio of usefulness was high. Before presuming to condemn Pierluigi for following the custom of his time, it may be well to ask ourselves if the spirit which prompted these courtier-like effusions is as dead now as were to be wished? More adroit it may be, less servile it certainly is, as the sense of humour has developed. Pomposity and long-windedness are elbowed out by rapid locomotion; "Your Highness's most obleeged" is as superannuated as the blunderbuss on Hampstead Heath. The man of genius and no

cash must find other and more subtle ways of
achieving that union between capital and labour
which forms the desired goal, but the probabilities
are that had he lived in the sixteenth century he
would not have found the slightest inconvenience
in comparing his patron to Phœbus Apollo, such
being the custom, and would have meant no more
by it than the more discreet and self-respecting
phrases in usage now.

Another letter to the Duke of Mantua is in
existence for the year following. Evidently
accompanying compositions, not specified, it is
interesting on account of a phrase Pierluigi
employs there—a reference to himself as *quasi
senili*, "getting old"; a reminder that he is now
fifty-nine and stands at the beginning of his last
decade. Nevertheless these were years yielding
some of his noblest compositions. In the same
letter he makes a playful reference to himself as
"il Palestina," showing that this quaint variation
of his name at the hands of the Duke's secretaries
had not escaped him.

Earlier in this year * Gregory XIII.'s pontificate came to an end. It was one of stirring
incidents, such as the war with the Turks, the
question of the Huguenots, the dispute over the
jurisdiction of the Church ; events in which, as a
loyal Churchman, Pierluigi certainly took deep

* 1585.

interest.   The inevitable political and social unrest attending the death of the Head of Christendom, the accompanying ceremonies—a matter of
personal import to the Master of the Julian
Chapel—to which by this time he was well
accustomed,* the uncertainty attending the election
of the new Pope ; all these factors indubitably
affected his life and work at this time.   At one
phase in the proceedings of the subsequent conclave
it seemed not unlikely that Cardinal Sirleto would
be elected as Gregory's successor.   From his
well-known interest in Church music it is to be
presumed that such an election would have been
favourable to the musicians, but the tide turned in
the direction of Cardinal Montalto, who, " elected
as an old man threw away his crutch, and he who
had before pretended incapacity, disease, old age,
and an almost timid complaisance was then at once
made active, vigorous, and haughty, and began to
exhibit his unheard-of ferocity." †   Unfortunately
for those who prefer a picturesque tale, this
account is as fantastic as that of Pierluigi's start
in life as a beggar-boy,‡ the truth being that
Sixtus V. was " a man in good health, active and
full of life ; nay, that he was still so vigorous and
in the full force of his years, is adduced as one of

* Gregory was the sixth Pope elected since Pierluigi's residence
in Rome.
† Ranke.
‡ Given by the older biographies.

the motives of his election"; an interesting
instance of varying points of view.

On the occasion when Sixtus made his ceremonial entry in St. Peter's it is on record that a
mass was sung composed expressly for the occasion
by Pierluigi, who had chosen for his theme the
subject from his motet with the title *Tu es Pastor
ovium;* but the choice of words was not sufficient
to ensure its approval by Sixtus, who is reported
to have compared the music unfavourably with
that of the Missa Papae Marcelli. Whether or
no this statement can be relied upon, at all events
Pierluigi was not dissatisfied with his mass, for he
included it shortly before his death in a volume
of others.   If his enemies rejoiced over the
Pope's adverse criticism, their triumph was short-
lived. *Tu es Pastor ovium* was followed by a
masterpiece of the first order. This is the famous
mass *Assumpta est Maria*, of which it is hard to
speak in sober terms. From the opening phrases
of the Kyrie the elevation of spirit, suavity, virgin
quality of sound, grip the hearer and convey the
instant conviction of greatness. It has been
remarked that Pierluigi must have had a special
veneration for the Queen of Heaven. Certain
is it that in all text relating to our Lord's mother
he employs what may be described as a certain
atmospheric quality, a purity, clarity of tone in
remarkable harmony with the attributes of the

Virgin-mother. An analysis of the mechanical means by which he achieves this reveals only a certain grouping of the voices, an inclination to employ the higher registers of these, thus creating an open, pulsating effect, very sweet and calm. In the *Gloria* he illustrates the passage *Tu solus altissimus* with an ascending passage culminating on the final word (in the part assigned to the first tenor) with the triumphant sweep upwards of an octave. The satisfying effect of this simple device is heightened by the apparently ingenuous scale-passage down which the voices proceed to the final "Amen." Its simplicity recalls the work of Fra Angelico, the more subtle in its power over the imagination by reason of its inherent quality of apparent candour. Attention may be called to this mass as a remarkable instance of Pierluigi's method of dividing the voices antiphonally. An instance occurs in the opening bars—in the first *Kyrie*—where two sopranos and the first tenor are grouped against contralto, second tenor, and bass. In this way he obtains that contrast of timbre which is so extraordinarily effective in a great space where resonance has free play. The first performance of this *chef a'œuvre* was on August 15, 1585, the Festival of the Assumption. It is said that so much haste was required to get it finished that Pierluigi left insufficient time for the copying of the voice-parts, resorting, at the last moment, to the printing-press from which, in five days, the first impression was issued, without date, composer's, or publisher's name. The ceremonies of the *festa* took place as usual in S. Maria Maggiore, and Sixtus is reported to have left the church smiling, remarking that the new mass could be from no other pen but Pierluigi's, an *amende honorable* perhaps if necessarily obvious. One of the results of this triumph may be identified in a curious affair, the threads of which are difficult to unravel. A few months later another attempt was made to include Pierluigi among the members of the Pontifical Choir, this time as *Maestro della Cappella.* Did Pierluigi desire it, or was the initiative to be sought elsewhere? Did Sixtus wish that the lustre of this great musician's name should be added to his official choir? The accounts are so deficient and so confused that it is impossible to arrive at a conclusion. The probabilities point to indiscreet action on the part of Pierluigi's admirers, roused, it may be, to enthusiasm by his latest masterpiece, for it is almost inconceivable that Pierluigi, who knew his Rome, should have placed himself in a position to be flouted by the Pontifical Choir. Here are the facts. The project was set on foot by a person unknown. A certain Monsignor Antonio Boccapadule undertook the office of go-between, and not the least remarkable part of the affair is that he himself was Master of the Choir, the very person, it might have been thought, interested in keeping Pierluigi out. This may be regarded as an argument for the theory advanced by some, that Sixtus himself had a hand in the matter, for who so well able to compensate Boccapadule for his self-abnegation? At first he proceeded in a diplomatic manner, canvassing the younger members of the choir. On finding that one of these, a certain Tommaso Benigni, was in favour of the scheme he commissioned this personage to sound the other members. His enthusiasm for the matter in hand appears to have misled him : possibly, indeed, the choir was backward in giving an opinion, not desiring without strong support to advance into the open. Benigni took this caution for assent, and from his account of the matter considered himself justified in calling a meeting at his house. To his astonishment opposition of the most determined character manifested itself, the members of the choir objecting—thus did history repeat itself—that Pierluigi was a layman and married. Boccapadule did not at once lose courage, possibly thinking the opposition would die down. This was not the case. A few days later a meeting was called at the Chapter-house, all the singers being present, and not only was the proposal quashed, but

Benigni was subjected to a severe reprimand and to a fine for introducing a measure he well knew to be contrary to the fundamental laws of his corporation. But according to Baini the matter did not rest here. Taking the view that Sixtus himself desired Pierluigi's election but did not wish to appear as prime mover in the project, knowing full well that it was not in accordance with the regulations—the Abbé proceeds to tell us that the Pope forthwith dismissed four singers in excess of the stipulated number, as if desiring to give an emphatic hint that such sticklers for the strict letter of the law as the Pontifical singers revealed themselves to be should set their house in order. True or not, one fact may with certainty be established. Shortly afterwards the official title of "Composer to the Pontifical Choir" was formally bestowed by the Pope on Pierluigi. This may be taken as a reparation for a painful affront, for it can scarcely be doubted that the affair was intensely disagreeable to the great musician. Thus his standing was defined and, though not actually a member, his new title gave him the coveted official position in the celebrated choir. As a coda to the proceedings, Sixtus, in the following year, issued a Bull confirming the pretensions of the Choir to elect their own Master from amongst themselves—one with fifteen years' service behind him, or failing that, the next in order of seniority. This might certainly be advanced as an argument against Baini's account that Sixtus had something to do with the scheme to make Pierluigi *Maestro della Cappella Pontificale.* In any case the singers vindicated their attitude and prevented any further attempt to tamper with their statutes.

Possibly in celebration of his new appointment, Pierluigi presented the Choir with two masses at this time : *Salve Regina* for five voices and *Ecce ego Joannes* for six. Ambros relates that little care was taken of the original manuscripts ; they were not, as was customary, copied into the great choir-books, and had not the choirmaster Orfei, after Pierluigi's death, put them into a safe place they would have been lost. As this cannot be attributed to ignorance it must be set down to jealousy of a peculiarly petty kind. If the world could have afforded to lose any of Pierluigi's works it would certainly not have been that most noble work *Ecce ego Joannes,* for although presenting points of contrast with the style of *Missa Papae Marcelli* and *Assumpta est Maria,* it reveals no diminution of strength, but rather a ripeness of conception, a philosophic cast of thought which stamp it as one of the greatest of his masses. It is evident that Pierluigi might dare to style himself *quasi senili,* for his intellectual vigour was worthy the envy of younger men.

His genius was of that order which time only ripens, and, until the end, there was to be no faltering in the stately procession of his works. The curious story is fairly typical of experiences common to every great man. Indeed, it may be argued that without these petty vexations fame cannot be considered as secure. Jealousy, conscious or unconscious, welcomes every opportunity of diminishing the success of a rival, and only great souls can resist its promptings or withstand its attacks. But the surmise may be permitted that Pierluigi had already acquired that serenity born of the conviction that brain and intellect have reached the goal for which every genius strives, that self-expression which brings its own reward.

CHAPTER XI

PIERLUIGI'S connection with the House of Gonzaga came to an end with the death of the Duke in the year 1587. His relations with William of Mantua had never been anything but créditable to them both ; on the one side the *connoisseur* capable of appreciating the greatness of the artist, on the other a dignified service for the favours received. Flattering as the phrases are in Pierluigi's dedications to his patron there is a ring of sincerity, for the artist perceives him capable of discrimination, and for that reason well worth serving. A study of the Mantuan records shows that the Duke's love of the arts was no mere accident. Very early in its history the Court of Mantua established its reputation as a centre of cultivation and learning, and William was not the first of his house to interest himself in the theories of composition. Amongst the archives for the year 1553 there exists an account of the performance of Ariosto's *I Suppositi,* the entr'actes for which were composed by

Cardinal Ercole Gonzaga,* regent of Mantua during Duke William's minority. Unfortunately none of the Duke's compositions, up to the present moment, have been traced, but entries in the Court accounts referring to the sending of music-paper from Venice, from the year 1560 onwards, correspond with the particulars of the Duke's compositions as revealed in his letters and serve to indicate this as no temporary whim but a serious and ardent study, to which he particularly applied himself (according to a statement in one of the letters) on those *villegiature* during the summer months which the notoriously unhealthy climate of Mantua rendered at this time imperative. In 1583 he sent a set of madrigals to the press, " not," as he quaintly explains, " through ambition, but that it be not labour lost," former works, it seems, having been lost, " and," he continues, " so as to be able to enjoy the fruits of past industry." Here is the measure of the man, intellectually humble, discerning, not to be cajoled by courtiers, conscious how hard it was for a prince to receive the benefit of honest criticism. These published madrigals are doubtless those of which he sent a copy to the Court of the Estes, also in the year 1583, and of which Ludovico

---

* It is truly astonishing that this most powerful Cardinal, who had a finger in every diplomatic pie in Europe, yet found time for the art of composition.

Agostino, its choirmaster and composer, writes as
follows : "The madrigals were sung in very good
company, and they caused every one who heard
them to marvel, not only through their excellence
but because they appeared worthy of imitation."
The latter part of the sentence may be taken as implying a certain amount of originality on the part
of the princely composer, or it may be a reference
to that *bello stifitio* and *spirito vivo alle parole* of
which Pierluigi speaks in the letter, already quoted,
of March 3, 1570. The Prince was noted for
his generosity, and not alone to his dependants,
one of his last acts being the gift of his Abbey of
Fellonico to the Pontifical Choir, to be used by
them as a place of relaxation and repose, the income from which was to remain at their disposal ;
a practical instance of his interest in all matters
affecting the musical portion of the Roman
Liturgy. While it is impossible to regret that
Pierluigi's life was not spent in the smaller world
of the Mantuan Court, it is highly probable that
it would have been calmer, freer from anxiety.
If, however, the point be considered objectively
it will be seen that here is, after all, only another
reason for satisfaction that Pierluigi remained in
Rome ; what great artist was ever the better for
freedom from those very cares which act as a
stimulus to his genius ?

The Mantuan correspondence continues to

within the last month of the Duke's life. The final letter, dated July 6, 1587, was from Pierluigi, written to introduce a certain Stefano Ugeri, a Cremonese, whose name is to be found in the Papal Choir lists from 1585 to 1591. He was the bearer of unnamed compositions from Pierluigi's pen, and the letter further informs the Duke that Ugeri is an inmate of his house, an interesting detail apparently warranting the assumption that Pierluigi admitted other musicians to his board beyond those he received in his official capacity as Master of the Julian Choir.* Or it may be read as a proof that he did, as Baini maintains, live in the choir-house at the entrance to the atrium of the old basilica, ostensibly intended for the Julian Choir but possibly capable of housing more than the regulation number of musicians attached to that foundation. Meagre as the reference is it is very welcome, for so little information can be gleaned as to Pierluigi's domestic circumstances. Thus this highly interesting correspondence closes, and Duke William of Mantua passes out of Pierluigi's life.

For one more detail of this year we turn to the archives of Palestrina, where it still remains on record that Pierluigi added yet another to the

---

* Between 1612 and 1615 Ugeri was Maestro di Cappella in the Pontifical choir.

vineyards he possessed there.* The guess may be hazarded that no summer passed without a sojourn in that place of cool and fragrant breezes so conveniently situated for the long *villegiature* essential to all persons residing in beautiful but insalubrious Rome. A tradition, indeed, exists that he spent much time there, honoured by his townsmen and surrounded by kinsfolk. A few of the latter may be established with certainty, the organist (since 1571) of S. Agapito, Cesare Veccia,† with others of that name ; Pierluigi's sister Palma, married to a burgher of the town in 1562, her celebrated brother, as head of the family, providing the indispensable dowry. Until 1581 his two grandchildren, Angelo's son and daughter, during their pathetically short lives, were much with their maternal grandfather, Pierluigi paying for their keep. Near enough for frequent visits, far enough to provide a pleasant haven of rest from the busy Roman life, the musician's birthplace must often have been in his thoughts. The lovely chains of hills around it were typical of those contrapuntal chains from which he wove his suave and ecstatic melodies ; the glories of a dying sunset over the *Campagnà* of those melting, sighing closes to a *Benedictus* or

* A similar purchase is recorded under the date of 1584.
† The Veccias were relations of his first wife, Lucrezia. In 1566 he placed two boys of that name, his nephews, in the Roman seminary.

Agnus Dei. Beauty enveloped him here, he had but to interpret its message—interpret, yet something more. Is not genius the critical faculty in man born of that Spirit which breathed over the beauty of the Creation and "saw that it was good"? Surely the "eyes to see" went with the "ears to hear" in Pierluigi's artist-nature so that he rested better in these surroundings than elsewhere. With the Psalmist he might have said, "O what great troubles and adversities hast Thou showed me, yet didst thou turn and refresh me, yea, and broughtest me from the deep of the earth again." And he could well have added, "Thou hast brought me to great honour and comforted me on every side." Where the capacity for suffering is great so is that for joy, and it is pleasant to think that, like a patriarch amongst his vines and olives, Pierluigi in Palestrina found this true.

His creative activity during the next few years was truly remarkable. It was as if he realized that his time was getting short, and wished to provide the Church he served so indefatigably with compositions for every conceivable ecclesiastical function. A fresh set of Lamentations, Magnificats, hymns, litanies, and offertories composed for the whole of the Church year succeeded each other. The inexhaustible riches of his imagination were never more apparent than in his treatment of the ancient plain-song melodies forming

the basis of these volumes, than in his freedom and
variety within the limits of a litany, hymn, or *Magnificat.* One word as to the Lamentations. These, the
only set published during his lifetime, were dedicated to the Pope, and this dedication is known
to all students of Pierluigi's life, as giving rise to
suppositions which, in the light of recent discovery,
no longer seem to be justified. In it he complains
bitterly of his poverty, the basis of Baini's view
as to the bad state of his finances. What, then,
was its true explanation ? Sixtus, a man of force-
ful character, was certainly not to be hoodwinked
by pleas of poverty designed to open his purse-
strings, and nothing we know of Pierluigi warrants
such a theory, though it has been freely advanced.
Probably Haberl is right when he surmises that
the great composer was thinking not only of the
splendid volumes which Orlandus Lassus, and Vittoria were able to bring out, but also of the large
quantity of his still unpublished works, not only
unpublished during his lifetime, but even remaining so until the end of the last century. In this
connection it is significant that not until his
marriage to a woman of considerable means was
he enabled to bring out fine editions. This fact
speaks for itself. After all, words are relative,
and Pierluigi was given to a certain picturesque
expression of his experiences, as may be deduced
already from the dedication to his first book of

masses (inscribed to Julius III.), and from his exaggerated repentance for those secular compositions so innocuous to modern eyes. In this instance he may have had hopes of persuading Sixtus into ordering a collected Vatican edition of the works of the " Composer to the Pontifical Choir," and if so, there was nothing extravagant in such an aspiration ; but the Pope, whose splendid architectural schemes were cribbed, cabined, and confined by the depressed state of the Pontifical exchequer, and who was notoriously in difficulties with regard to the funds for the completion of the new basilica, remained deaf to the hint, and Pierluigi gained nothing by his outburst.

Sixtus died in August. The five years of his active reign brought about many changes in Rome, and Pierluigi was now able to walk into the new cathedral and marvel at the mighty enterprise. Here is a contemporary account of its state at the moment of the Pope's death. Though still unfinished, " the great dome and the smaller dome, and also the enclosure which they call the greater chapel, together with other smaller chapels, and the whole building of the new church dedicated to St. Peter the Apostle" were in existence.* This was *the great fact* of Pierluigi's life and, in some aspects, must have appeared

* Cardinal Santaseverino (Ranke's translation).

more astounding then than now, as there was
no façade to conceal the extraordinary size
of its proportions as it rose, symmetrical and
dominating, from the mass of scaffolding and
half-ruined buildings a portent of the new
epoch.

Another period of uncertainty and unrest
followed the great Pope's death. His successor,
Urban VII., did not survive his election more
than a fortnight. A fresh conclave was immediately called, but an immense time was consumed
in deliberations, and it was not before December 5
that Cardinal Ugo Buoncompagni of Bologna
assumed the tiara as Gregory XIV. Gorgeous
ceremonial, stately Requiem, alternating with the
street-rows which invariably attended the election
of the Pontiff, *Te Deums* and shouts of *Evviva il
Papa* centred around the spot where Pierluigi
had his dwelling—namely, the precincts of the
Vatican—from which he concluded in this year
the purchase of a vineyard in the neighbourhood
of Rome.* Unfortunately, the document which
substantiates this statement merely states "in
his house by St. Peter's," so we are no wiser
than we were before. Earlier in the year he
again added to his possessions in Palestrina, buy-
ing a garden, stable, and certain plots of land.

One of Gregory XIV.'s first official acts affected

* Haberl.

Pierluigi pleasantly enough—the augmentation of the salaries of the Pontifical Choir, amongst whom was included their Composer. Just before this, a fifth book of masses made its appearance, containing the exquisite little *Iste Confessor* and the equally well-known *Æterna Christi munera.* It was dedicated to Duke William of Bavaria,* the generous patron of Lassus. There is no record of any acknowledgment from the Duke of this dedication, which was possibly prompted by a desire on Pierluigi's part to show himself in friendly rivalry with Lassus. Once again a mass may be mentioned constructed on a secular theme, *Nasce la gioia mia.* Baini is at great pains to explain this away, dwelling on the fact that Lassus had done the same thing, but, as has already been pointed out, Pierluigi was indifferent to the letter of the law if the substance was respected ; relying on his skill in transforming the material. Immediately after the appearance of this volume he brought out the Magnificats already referred to, dedicated to Gregory XIV. They appeared only a few days before that Pontiff's death, which occurred on October 15, 1591.

The events of the previous year now repeated themselves. Innocent IX. was elected, only to die on the last day but one of the year. A conclave sat throughout the whole of January, at the

---

* He succeeded Duke Albert, his father, in 1579.

end of which time Cardinal Ippolito Aldobrandini was chosen, and seated himself on the Papal throne as Clement VIII., bringing about the curious co-incidence that Pierluigi's life was spanned between the reigns of Clement VII. and Clement VIII. No fresh works were issued from the press during this year, for which Baini accounts by an illness, though on what evidence does not appear. In the following year the afore-mentioned Offertories and two volumes of Litanies were published, the first of these dedicated to a new patron, a French-man of noble family, the Abbé de Baume, a fer-vent admirer of the Master at this period, who gave him cause for warm expressions of gratitude. Simultaneously another patron appears, the young Cardinal Pietro Aldobrandini, a nephew of the Pope, who had been trained in that order of Oratorians which owed its foundation to S. Filippo. To this young man Pierluigi dedicated his sixth book of masses, containing *Dies sanctificatus; In te Domine speravi;* his second mass with the title *Sine Nomine,* concealing a fresh employment of a secular theme "Je suis deshéritée " ; *Quam pulchra es*—for four voices—and *Dilexi quoniam,* for five. While these were yet in the press Pierluigi dedi-cated a book of *madrigali spirituali* to the wife of Ferdinando de' Medici, Grand Duke of Tuscany, who, originally a Cardinal, succeeded on the death of his brother to the Grand Duchy, and, relinquishing his Cardinalate, married, never having taken vows.

These are the last works of which Pierluigi actually superintended the publication, though a seventh book of masses was already sent to be printed when he was seized with violent illness. This was an attack of pleurisy on January 26, 1594, from which his enfeebled constitution was unable to rally. Baini gives many touching details of these last sad days, of which, however, no corroboration can be found. That Pierluigi was, as he asserts, supported during his illness by his friend S. Filippo Neri has only probability in its favour, but if so, he was in the best of hands. He who had instituted the Order for the contemplation of celestial things by means of musical harmonies could understand, could help, as no other. And when the light grew dim and the world receded, surely the dying musician heard in the gathering darkness harmonies more supernal, more ravishing, than any finding their way to earth through his brain and hand—" the voices of harpers harping with their harps ; and they sung as it were a new song before the throne, and before the four beasts, and the elders ; and no man could learn that song but the hundred and forty and four thousand which were redeemed from the earth."

The boy-genius from the Sabine hills had done his work. Step by step, emerging from obscurity to fame, he bore music aloft and taught it to express all that the tongue dare not utter, because such emotion, such ecstasy, is too great for words defiled by common use. Now silence was there.

CHAPTER XII

PIERLUIGI was buried, according to custom, on the day he died. His body was enclosed in a plain coffin with a leaden plate, on which was inscribed—

JOANNES PETRUS ALOYSIUS PRAENESTINUS,
MUSICAE PRINCEPS.

That the funeral rites were performed with all possible honour and dignity can be established from contemporary accounts. Here is one from the *Puntatore* or Registrar of the Pontifical Choir—

"February 2, 1594.—This morning died the most excellent musician, Signor Giovanni Pierluigi, our dear companion, and *Maestro di Cappella* at St. Peter's Church, whither his funeral was attended not only by all the musicians of Rome, but by an infinite concourse of people, when *Libera me Domine* was sung by the whole College."

Another account adds the detail that *Libera me Domine* was sung to his setting, a five-part psalm for three choirs.* According to Baini, the

* For other account see Torrigio, *Le Sacre Grotte Vaticane.*

distance from the choir-school being so short, the
coffin was first carried round the Borgo, thus
giving sufficient space for the marshalling of the
long procession, divided into three sections by
the chanting choirs. It is to be regretted that
the *Puntatore* did not give more details, if only
for the reason that the mere enumeration of names
would have served to supply certain deficiencies
in the life-histories of some of the best-known
of these musicians of Rome. For instance, did
Vittoria, he who loved the dead musician so
greatly as to fashion his clothing on his, follow the
Master ? Was Marenzio there ? or was he still
in the Court of Poland, a prized and honoured
guest ? But though these questions must remain
unanswered, there is enough to show it was a
great funeral pageant ; the bier borne high on
stalwart shoulders, between lines of sandalled
friars grasping dripping, flaring candles and chanting the Prayers for the Dead as they go ; the
Pontifical choir ; the Julian choir; the " Company
of Rome," mourning their brightest "jewel" ; a
great concourse of friends—S. Filippo certainly
amongst these, with the last sad scenes at the
bedside fresh in his mind ; the crowd, made up
of every conceivable element ; the Swiss guards
(in the picturesque dress designed for them by
Michelangelo) keeping order—difficult enough in
these narrow streets of the Borgo, but easier as

the long procession breaks into the great space
of the piazza.   Here the voices of the singers
would achieve their greatest effect, supported by
the impressive tolling of St. Peter's bells cele-
brating, with mournful clang, the passing of their
colleague in the service of the Sanctuary, on his
final progress to the ancient basilica.

*Libera me Domine de morte aeterna in die illa
tremenda,* the beautiful mournful chant was Pierluigi's last prayer as his body descended to the
dust.

In the *Liber Mortuorum Parochiae S. Peter de
urbe inceptus die prima Januarii* 1545—that is to
say, the parish-book of interments in the Church
of St. Peter, the following entry occurs : *A di
2 Feb.* 1594 *Messer Gio. Lui. da Palestrina maestro
di cappella di S. Pietro sepolto alla cappella nova.*
This perfectly plain statement in appearance conceals a mystery, for at the present moment no one
knows where the body of Pierluigi rests.   For
this reason : when Julius II. (1503) determined
to build a magnificent tomb for himself he
abandoned his first idea of adding a chapel to
the existing church which, it was found, was in a
crumbling condition, and decided to carry out
the scheme favoured by his predecessor Nicholas
V. of constructing an entirely new edifice.   His
first act was to build a transverse wall shutting
off a little more than half the basilica ; the larger

OLD ST. PETER'S, PARTIALLY DEMOLISHED WITH THE NEW BUILDING RISING BEHIND. AS SEEN IN 1535

Martin van Heemskerck

half being known in future as the *basilica nuova*
or new church, the smaller half, which continued
to be used for its sacred purposes as before, as the
basilica vecchia or old church. In the *basilica
nuova* all the ancient chapels were demolished and
the bones of those buried there transferred to
a recently discovered vault under the round
chapel of St. Petronilla, formerly outside the
walls of ancient St. Peter's, but now included in
the scheme of the building about to be erected.
In Paul III.'s reign (1534) in consequence of the
collapse of a wall in the old building, the Sacrament-altar was reinstated in the chapel of St.
Simon and St. Jude, situated between the fifth
and sixth columns of the old basilica which the
authorities proceeded to adorn very richly with
precious marbles, paintings and gilding. From
henceforth this chapel was known as the Cappella
Nuova or New Chapel. There Pierluigi was
buried.*   In the subsequent reign of Paul V.
(1605) it was decreed that the old church (*basilica
vecchia*) should forthwith be taken down, and
therefore the Sacrament-altar was transferred once
more ; this time to the other side of the transverse wall, the *basilica nuova*, where the finished
chapel erected by Gregory XIII., and for that
reason known as the Gregorian Chapel, was ready
to receive it. The bodies of St. Simon and St.

* His wife, Lucrezia, was also buried in the Cappella Nuova.

Jude were transferred to a chapel prepared for
them on the left side of the new cathedral on the
site of the former chapel of St. Petronilla which
now received the name Chapel of St. Simon and
St. Jude. While engaged in the necessary ex-
cavations the workmen found another vault or
receptacle in the neighbourhood of the first and
to this all the bones and coffins left in the *basilica
vecchia* were now brought, amongst them, it is
supposed, those of Pierluigi. The vergers to-day
point with certainty to a space in front of the
present altar of St. Simon and St. Jude as
Pierluigi's grave ; but when this spot was opened
in conformity with certain investigations carried
out in 1914,* no coffin of the *Musicae Princeps* was
found. If it be considered that twelve years had
already elapsed since Pierluigi was buried in the
Cappella nuova of the *basilica vecchia,* that he was
moved with a vast quantity of other remains to
his new resting-place, and by workmen, it is not
altogether a matter of surprise that this doubt
exists ! It was largely a contractor's job, not
necessarily implying any lack of order or decency
—though there are historical instances where the
results have been equally unfortunate ; as for
example : the body of Pope Urban VI., tossed
out of its sarcophagus so that this receptacle
might be filled with water for moistening the

* By Dr. Ludwig von Pastor.

mortar employed in the new building of St. Peter's ; or—a case very much nearer our own time—of Mozart thrown into a common grave without even a friend standing by to mark the site.

To return once more to Pierluigi's funeral ceremonies. On February 14 a Requiem Mass was performed to his memory, sung in the chapel of S. *Maria del Soccorso* in the *basilica nuova ;* this was the chapel to which the body of St. Gregory Nazianzen had been transferred with so much pomp in 1580, the occasion on which Pierluigi composed the two motets included later in the volume dedicated to Cardinal Andreas Bathory. If, therefore, pilgrims to the tomb of the great musician are foiled in their pious purpose, they may instead cross the great nave to the Chapel of the *Madonna del Soccorso* and reconstruct for themselves this last act of devotion to Pierluigi's memory.

The farewell mention of Pierluigi's name in the Choir-books concerns the final payment to his son and heir, Igino, of his monthly salary. Shortly afterwards the book which Pierluigi had already delivered to the printers—the seventh volume of masses—appeared, with a dedication to Clement VIII. penned by Igino. Under the date March 1 he informs His Holiness that his father charged him, during the last moments of his life, with the publication of all his remaining manuscripts ; that it was his intention to fulfil this charge as his means gave him opportunity, in which filial duty he humbly hoped for the assistance of the Holy Father.

It cannot be denied that the character of Igino is subsequently shown in anything but a favourable light, as that of a man devoted, at any cost, to the task of making money. At the same time, to describe him as an " unprincipled scoundrel," a " wild and worthless man," is to stretch the facts to breaking point. The tangled skein of the *Graduale* reappears to confuse the evidence against him, and it becomes exceedingly difficult to distinguish facts from mere accusations. Before giving an account of these transactions it is only fair to suggest that part of Igino's unworthy conduct may have been actuated by a sentiment of resentment against the Vatican authorities, prompting him to dispose of his father's manuscripts outside Rome rather than have any further dealings with them. While, however, going so far in his defence, it would be easy to find harder terms for his bad management of his father's affairs and for the little consideration he showed for his father's posthumous dignity. For this it is impossible to forgive him.

A few months before Pierluigi's death, he was approached by a certain Leonardo Parasoli, who invented a form of musical type, of unusually large size, in which he proposed to print a revision of the Gradual and Antiphonary. In this scheme he desired to enlist Pierluigi's services, not only for the sake of his great reputation but as a means of persuading the Vatican to countenance the proceeding which the Medicean printing house (of which Parasoli was an employé) was to carry through. Apparently Pierluigi showed no disinclination to forward the enterprise, for which he was offered the handsome sum of 800 sc. There was the already completed work lying by, the whole of the Temporale, useless since the abandonment of the former project undertaken at the instance of Gregory XIII., and probably a quantity of half-completed material ; rendering the present one a very different proposition from that made earlier, which entailed an enormous amount of research and time—expenditure without any corresponding pecuniary advantage. But death intervened. How much of the work was already completed it is impossible to say. Igino now resolved to turn the affair to his advantage. He began by asking twice as much as his father had done, and in order to do this he obviously represented the work as finished. Even then the publishers did not withdraw, having reason to hope that the Sacred Congregation of Rites would enjoin the use of the new Gradual and Antiphonary on the faithful throughout Christendom.

Not finally rejecting the idea, the Congregation nevertheless hesitated to enforce conformity in this drastic way, though, on March 29, they were pressed into the admission that it was desirable all non-conformity should cease in the celebration of the offices; whereupon the publishers decided to proceed. But Igino made one excuse after the other for not delivering his father's manuscript, and eight months elapsed before it passed into the publishers' hands. The next step was to submit it to the Sacred Congregation of Rites, who imposed this condition on the publishers before giving a partial sanction to publication. Upon this Igino made an outcry, complaining that the Congregation were not competent to criticize his father's work. Suspicions were aroused. The manuscript was shown to experts who declared that the *Sanctorale* could not possibly be by Pierluigi, that it was full of mistakes and inaccuracies. Nor was this all. Thoroughly suspicious by this time of the whole transaction, the Sacred Congregation of Rites refused their permission for the appearance of the work. The publishers naturally withdrew from their contract with Igino and desired to return the manuscript which he refused to receive, demanding payment of the sum agreed on. The result was a lawsuit which dragged on interminably. In the end Igino could neither enforce payment, nor would he accept the return of the manuscript, which actually found its way to the Mont-de-piété where it still remained at Igino's death. It was only taken out in 1610 by order of Paul V., who gave it into the hands of Anerio and Soriano. They edited it as the *Editio Medicaea,* published in the year 1614. As may readily be imagined, this disagreeable affair put the Vatican thoroughly on their guard against Igino and if—as Baini states—the Pope seriously contemplated bringing out a complete edition of Pierluigi's works, he may well have hesitated before committing himself to dealings with the great composer's son. On Igino's side, he saw no great chances of profit, was in a very bad temper over the failure of his schemes, and in order to save himself expense in publishing, also possibly to annoy the Vatican, he sold the remainder of his father's manuscripts to two Venetians, Tiberio de Argentis and Andrea de Agnetis, who proceeded to edit volume after volume of hitherto unpublished masses ; brought out with one exception by the Venetian house of Scoto, this remaining book receiving publication at the hands of Amadino of Venice. The works were arranged in the following order :—

Volume 8.—1599.

Quem dicunt homines ;
Dum esset summus pontifex ;
O admirable commercium (from the beauti-
ful motet of that name) ;
Memor esto ;
Dum complerentur ; and
Sacerdotes Domini.

Volume 9.—1599.

Ave Regina coelorum ;
Veni sponsa Christi ;
Vestiva i colli (based on Pierluigi's mad-
rigal of the same name) ;
Sine nomine ;
In te Domine speravi ; and
Te Deum laudamus.

Volume 10.—1600.

In illo tempore ;
Già fu chi m'vèbbe cara ;
Petra sancta ;
O Virgo simil et mater ;
Quinti toni ; and
Illumina oculos meos.

The last-mentioned mass, based on a theme
taken from a motet composed by André de Silva,
and which figures in a fanciful account of the
rescue of Church music as related by Baini, had
already appeared in the second edition of the

seventh volume published by Coattino of Rome,
under the title *Ad bene placitum.*

Volume 11.—1600.
Descendit Angelus Domini;
Regina coeli;
Quando lieta;
Octavi toni; and
Alma redemptoris.

Volume 12.
Regina coeli;
O rex gloriæ;
Ascendo ad patrem;
Qual è il più gran' amor;
Tu es Petrus; and
Viri Galilei.

The thirteenth volume contained four masses,
the last of which had already been published.
They were respectively :—

1601.
Laudate Dominum;
Hodie Christus natus est (both taken from
    motets with similar titles) ;
Fratres ego enim accepi; and
Confitebor.

Surely this long list of works waiting for
publication must have weighed heavily on Pierluigi as his last hours ebbed.   In spite of his
great reputation, of the wide recognition of his

genius, he knew that an immense number of his best compositions (far from being completed by this list) were at the mercy of circumstances— loss, neglect, or wilful destruction. "I have been a poor man all my life," was true in this sense. What if he had housing, clothes, food, and to spare! These children of his brain were unhoused, unclothed, and he had to die leaving them so. He was probably aware of the deficiencies of his son and to what poor hands he was consigning his manuscripts. There is at least some cause for thankfulness that, in the result, it was no worse and that to the Venetians fell the credit of publishing such sublime and delightful works as *Dum complerentur* and *O admirabile commercium*. The four-part interlude in the *Gloria* of the former—*Domine Fili unigenite Jesu Christe, Domine Deus, Agnus Dei, Filius Patris* —is one of the most inspired moments in any of Pierluigi's works and constitutes in itself a supreme act of worship ; as if the angels themselves veiled their faces with their wings as they recited the titles of " the Lamb worthy to be slain."

Let us now take leave of Igino. The best that can be said for him is that he has not given his account of the matter ; the worst, that he was the unworthy son of a great father. Yet, from the latter point of view, there seems a little incongruity in the close of his life, for it is related of

him that, after losing his wife, he took orders and
was made a canon of S. Agapito in his father's
native town to which he retired for his remaining
years. But he only enjoyed this position twenty-
one days, dying in 1610. Of his children there
is no further mention. The direct line of descendants came to an end in or after 1677.

CHAPTER XIII

(*Concluding remarks*)

AFTER the issue of the thirteenth volume of masses this wonderful stream of compositions was stemmed. It is true there was a reprint, in a mutilated form, of three masses in 1619 with subsequent re-edition until 1689 ; motets also, and hymns constantly reappeared, but until the advent of the great collected edition at the end of the last century no hitherto unpublished composition by Pierluigi saw the light. The Roman School was virtually dead and the signs of the times were there for all to read when it became possible to bring out arrangements of compositions originally *a cappella* with instrumental accompaniments. An accompaniment implies harmony. The chord became of paramount importance, that is, the sound combination formed by the organized contact of many voices. One of the first things a student of counterpoint is called upon to learn is to consider his melody or voice-part horizontally, while the student of harmony must regard his from a perpendicular point of view, each junction of the voices forming a dissonance or consonance which must be approached and quitted according to rule. The moment instruments were employed to accompany part-singing the perpendicular chord was all important, the strong and weak beat controlled the accents and a certain quality of indefiniteness which was as the very breath of the unaccompanied polyphonic school was gone for ever. Paradoxical as it may seem, modern music, while gaining in subtlety, colouring and weight, has lost in *size*. An unaccompanied six-part mass (obviously there is no restriction in the multiplication of voices) is practically immeasurable, for it is confined in no limit of rhythmic beat, thematic structure, or chromatic formula. Not that there is no beat, no structure, no key-scheme ; such a course would result in chaos ; but the beat is not limited by regularly recurring bar-lines, or the structure by fixed patterns—if the expression be allowed—of development. Again, the chromatic formula is that peculiar to the ecclesiastical modes, which, as already pointed out, differed fundamentally from our modern scale system and particularly as to the treatment of the "full close" or point of repose. The uniformity of *timbre* through the sole employment of the human voice, the absence of percussion, or of violent changes of any sort, create a certain atmosphere on which the spirit floats. To borrow a simile from architecture— it is unlikely that any one could enter the Pantheon in Rome without a sudden and startling sense of the vast space. Reflection alone reveals the art hidden in the cunning gradations of the enormous dome, the coffering of which directs the vision to the limitless vault beyond as seen through the circular opening in the centre. In other words, there is no apparent standard by which to gauge the proportions of the whole. In Pierluigi's music there is the same absence of a definite point of comparison by which to measure, and if the score be examined this seems even more remarkable, as nothing in the disposition of the voices would lead one to anticipate this quality of infinite space, this effect of divine freedom. There is something inexpressibly quietening in these "exquisite rhythms," for time and space fall away and with them the contemplation of earthly things. But appreciation of these heavenly chains of melody does not necessarily imply regret that the modern development of music took the course it did. Such a postulate would be merely ridiculous, for, as the sense of individual consciousness and responsibility grew, the selfless, passionless music of the Roman School ceased to express it. Actuality, at all events in some measure, can never be dispensed with if art is to be living.

Still, while conceding so much to modernity, it is a matter for regret that musicians have so often failed to perceive the innate divergence of religious and secular ideals. The Latin races, particularly, have sinned in this respect, and even to-day, in spite of a determined effort towards purification, it is possible to visit churches celebrated for the beauty of their music and to hear *O salutaris hostia* sung with exactly the same sentiment and colouring as would be suitable in a performance of the Preislied. And it may be added that ninety-nine people out of a hundred will murmur "how beautiful," and think they are listening to Church music. Yet, strange to say, at least fifty out of that hundred will readily perceive the exaggerations and distortions of sentiment in the post-renaissance schools of painting, the influences which killed, though very much more slowly, those qualities of self-restraint and physical quiescence which are necessary to a truly religious form of musical art. In this wide generalization it is impossible to particularize, or to consider the influence exercised by the masterpieces of Johann Sebastian Bach on Church music. The assertion that the element of dramatic expression, although confined to a stern and intellectual realism, nevertheless constituted a fall from those spheres of pure contemplation to which Pierluigi conducts us, should be substantiated by careful comparison of corresponding passages for which there is no opportunity here.

What the course of music in the West might have been if the influences of the Roman School had not been arrested by the instant and overwhelming success of opera may be surmised if the corresponding line of expansion be considered in Russia. The marvellous vitality and freedom from convention in that most interesting national school may be, in no small measure, attributed to the hold unaccompanied polyphony retained over the minds of the people. They passed from one musical formula to the other without experiencing successive stages. That is to say, when they, very much later in time, conceived the idea of writing opera, they brought to bear on it artistic experiences inspired by a true polyphonic tradition. It only became necessary to add the strongly-marked rhythms of their characteristic dances, and their school of national opera received its distinctive features. Such a result was only possible in a country where a national conservatism went hand in hand with a comparative isolation from western modes of thought and where a process of evolution was superseded, or very much curtailed, by a most remarkable intellectual intuition.* It may seem strange enough to those

* In Moscow and Petrograd there were choirs until recently whose singing *alla cappella* must have closely resembled the finest standard of sixteenth-century art

brought up in the Classical and Romantic School created around the glorious names of musical literature, that so much insistence should be made on a more or less bygone form of art. To these the contention that anything has been lost in the supersession of ancient ideals by methods of chromatic development, thematic expansion, and pyschological expression would be simply foolish. And there is nothing to cause astonishment in this point of view. The secrets of the great schools of painting, and the influence they exercised, may be sought for on the walls of a museum or art gallery, but the opportunities of making acquaintance with the masterpieces of a remote musical past are indeed few and far between. And it may safely be said that he who trusts to an instrument of percussion for the reproduction of these melodic chains will not be indisposed to say, " Let the dead past bury its dead," for it will be to him as a very valley of dead bones. The contrapuntal art may indeed astonish him, but the suavity, purity, and spirituality of invention cannot be conveyed by these means. Fortunately, if rare, there are other and better ways, as more and more attention is now being given to this ancient school, and in no capital of Europe may they be heard to better advantage than in London, in the appropriate atmosphere and spirit.*

* At Westminster Cathedral.

Although the Roman School was deposed from its great position by the overpowering craving for dramatic expression and ornament, it was inevitable that, sooner or later, an attempt should be made to reinstate it. Possibly the first to call the attention of his countrymen to the works of the school in general and of Pierluigi in particular, was Dr. Burney,* who writes in these unmistakable, if quaint, terms : " It is hoped that no apology will be necessary for the length of the article " (on the Roman School), "which the reader can make as short as he pleases. . . . In a general history of Ancient Poetry Homer would doubtless occupy the most ample and honourable place, and Palestrina, the Homer of the most Ancient Music that has been preserved, merits all the reverence and attention which it is in a musical historian's power to bestow." But Burney's voice was that of one, more or less, crying in the wilderness, for the world had grown indifferent and the psychological moment had not yet come. The century-glass turned once again and the Abbé Baini took up the burden, but he wrote for his countrymen and Northerners had no opportunity of hearing the works, which, to do him justice, he reproduced with so much zeal and enthusiasm in the services of the Sistine Chapel. The Englishman

---

* Burney published in his "History of Music" the celebrated *Stabat Mater*, the *Improperia*, and the motet *Fratres ego enim accepi*.

who arrived in Rome for Passion-week in his travelling-coach with courier and men-servants was not frequently the clay of which musicians are made, and even if he enjoyed a passion for the art, the idiom was coldly unfamiliar. With the rich, warm, *fioritura* and Southern fire of the operatic singer most in vogue at the moment ringing in his ears, what was he likely to make of a form of music for which pre-eminently one must possess the "ear to hear"? Then the Germans intervened, primarily from a sense of the degradation into which ecclesiastical music had fallen; for no one who had studied the history of Church music could fail to perceive that the abuses complained of by the Council of Trent were almost all common features of the day. Dr. Karl Proske, priest and scholar, devoted himself to its purification, and very wisely went to the source from whence the waters flowed crystal clear; for which reason his tombstone records him as *Musicae divinae restaurator ingeniosissimus.* In the prosecution of this intention he visited Rome in the year 1834, and the diary of this journey constitutes one of the most interesting accounts extant of the state of Church music at that time. On November 1, 3, and 4 respectively, he heard a performance in the Sistine Chapel of Pierluigi's *Missa Brevis* and *Requiem*, in S. Carlo al Corso, his *Aeterna Christi munera*, serving to show that Baini, still active though already in ill-health, had succeeded to some extent in reinstating the works of the *Musicae Princeps*. But the difficulties experienced by Proske in fulfilling his object—that of cataloguing the unpublished works of the great period—were well-nigh prohibitive. Jealous suspicion alternated with crass indifference, forming an almost insuperable barrier. With patience and tact he partially overcame his difficulties. His catalogue reveals, under the circumstances, a triumphant result, containing as it does the whole of the masses contained in the 11, 12, 13, 15, 16, and 22 volumes of the Breitkopf and Härtel edition, as well as a miscellaneous collection of smaller works constituting in themselves a formidable achievement. Thus the way was marked out and followed by such men as Dr. Franz Xaver Witt, the founder of the Society of St. Cecilia, Espagne, Theodore de Witt, Franz Commer, Bauerle, and last, but not least, by Haberl. He it was who gathered up the labours of his forerunners into the gigantic enterprise of a collected edition completed on the three hundredth anniversary of the great musician's death, with the co-operation of subscribers in England, France, Holland, Austria, Germany, and Italy. This naturally dwarfs all other efforts, such as those of Choron and the Prince of la Moskowa, or of the yet more important services

of the Choir of St. Gervais in Paris, the Bach
Choir, and other societies in England. The
celebrations in connection with the tri-centenary
all over the world, and notably in Rome, helped
to advertise the revival, and since that time a
growing interest has been quickened by the *motû
proprio* of Pius X., issued on November 22, 1903,
who, in this document, insisted on a return to
the plainsong melodies of the Primitive Church
coupled with those works of the Roman School
that "agree so well with it." * But the obstacles
are still many. The Israelites could not make
bricks without straw, and the churches cannot
produce choirs capable of coping with the difficulties of *alla cappella* singing without money,
which means good training and good voices.
Very considerable spade-work remains before
those interested in restoring this great beauty to
the churches at large. It is not, indeed, only a
matter of money but of education, and that is
perhaps the hardest part of all.

* It should perhaps be mentioned that the ultimate results of
Pius X.'s *motû proprio* was to discredit the whole of the Ratisbon
publications in favour of the purer art of Solesmes ; but this only
refers to plainsong.

CHAPTER XIV

(*Concluding Remarks—continued*)

AN allusion was made in the preceding chapter to the tri-centenary festival in 1894. In 1914 a curious scheme was set on foot in Palestrina to celebrate the four hundredth anniversary of the great townsman's birth, thus postulating its occurrence in 1514.* In the opening chapters dealing with the early life it was considered inadvisable to check the flow of the narrative at that point with an inquiry into the various dates assigned by different authors to this interesting fact, but it is obvious that no book pretending to deal with Pierluigi's history can afford to ignore the controversy which rages round this question. The statement was made that he was born towards the end of 1525, but the dates given by the best known authorities range from 1514 to 1529. The first of these has still many adherents, particularly in Palestrina where it has attained to the force of a tradition—

* A statue was unveiled there in October, 1921.

hence the project just referred to. It is founded on the inscription discovered on that portrait of Pierluigi formerly in the Quirinal, now in the Sixtine Chapel. This runs: *Joannes Petrus Aloysius Praenestinus Musicae Princeps, sub Julio III. prius cantor, mox sub Pio IV., modulator pontificius, lateranae et liberianae, demum bis vaticanae basilicae capellae magister. Obiit IV. Idus Februarii MDXCIV.* vixit prope octogenarius; sepultus est sub Sacello vaticano St. Simonis et Judae.* This is authoritative enough ; but it has *now* been established that the handwriting is later in date than the portrait, corroborated by the circumstance that it was unknown to Andrea Adami, writing in 1711. But until this fact was discovered, the inscription was regarded as authoritative, coinciding, as it did, with the statement made by Igino in the dedication of the seventh book of masses to Clement VIII. : *Joannes Petraloysius pater meus septuaginta fere vitae suae annos in Dei laudibus componendi consumens. . . .†* It was pointed out that Pierluigi probably went into the choir of St. Agapito at the age of ten, thus entering on the service of " nearly seventy years " to which Igino refers. On the other hand, Baini took Igino's statement literally, even the qualifying

* " . . . He lived to be nearly eighty." The rest of the inscription is taken up with his various appointments, etc., etc.

† Giovanni Pierluigi, my father, spent nearly seventy years of his life in composing to God's praise.

fere receiving scant attention. Thus, seventy
years subtracted from 1594 left the date 1524;
so Pierluigi was, on the evidence of his son,
indubitably born in 1524. Round these central
positions most biographers ranged themselves,
though yet others selected the year 1520—based
on the ground of certain *Memorie incerte* de-
posited by Baini in the archives of the Sixtine
Chapel after the publication in 1826 of his
*Memorie storicocritiche della vita e delle opere di
Giovanni da Palestrina*, or 1529, the date chosen
by Adami, who as the oldest writer on Pierluigi
was supposed to be the most reliable. Haberl
himself accepted the date 1514 after investigations
he was able to make on the spot (in Palestrina),
but was first shaken, then convinced, this time
irrevocably, by finding another inscription on the
last sheet of the tenor-part in a volume of French
masses. Written in an educated hand was the
following : . . . Cum igitur hec omnia Musicae
munera nemo his temporibus melius Prenestino
nostro prestiterit, Iure optimo Musicae parentem
ut homerum poeticae possumus nominare. Mori-
tur mense februarij die purificationis beate
Mariae virginis Anno virginei partus 1594.
Sedente Clemente P.P. VIII. Fuit sepultus in
dicta Basilica maxima cum pompa funerali et
magna cantorum comitante caterva et qui vidit
hec scripsit Melchior major. Vixit annis LXVIIJ.

Ut re mi fa sol la ascendunt, sic peruia coelos
Transcendit volitans nomen ad astra tuum (o Prenestine).

O mors inevitabilis, mors amara et improba, mors
crudelis, que templa dulcibus sonis privas et aulas
principum, Prenestinum dum necasti, illum nobis
abstulisti, qui suam per armoniam illustravit ec-
clesiam ; Propterea tu Musicae dic requiescat in
pace. Melchioris sum.*

Thus, for the first time, a definite statement
was made by a contemporary which corroborated
the figurative sentence in Igino's dedication, for
the latter was not meant to be taken literally ; it
was a poetic statement, approximately true, such
as is often made in similar cases.

At first Dr. Haberl scarcely seems to have
realized the importance of his find. Who, then,
was Melchior ? † On what grounds should his
statement be accepted as final ? Dr. Haberl
spent two years over the uncertainty. But the

---

* Which, freely translated, runs—
Therefore, as our Palestrina was before all others in our times
in the display of all these gifts of music he may truly be called the
Father of Music, as was Homer of Poetry. He died in the month
of February, on the Purification of the B. V. Mary, A.D. 1594, in
the reign of Clement VIII., and was buried in the aforementioned
great basilica (St. Peter's) with funeral pomp and accompanied by
a great body of singers, as he who writes this, Melchior Major,
witnessed.

> Ut, re, mi, fa, sol, la ascends, and in like manner
> Rises thy name to the stars, O Palestrinian.

O miserable Death, Death bitter and horrible, cruel Death, who
robbeth the temples and the halls of the princes of such sweet sounds
in slaying Palestrina, thou hast also taken from us one who glorified
the Church by his harmony, therefore bid music, rest in peace.

† See Appendix, G. P. da P. Casimiri, p. 36.

internal evidence was too strong. It had everything in its favour ; Pierluigi's extraordinary intellectual vigour between the years 1584 and
1594—astonishing enough in a man of sixty to
seventy, almost incredible in a man of seventy to
eighty ; his willingness to abandon Rome for the
service of the Duke of Mantua—an improbable
decision had he been in reality over seventy, but
by no means unusual at sixty ; even the fact of
his remarriage—the step being much more natural
at sixty than at seventy,—all these circumstances
corroborate the accuracy of the date. But certainly the strongest link in the chain of evidence
is afforded by the fact that Pierluigi's first published madrigal, *Con dolce altiera*, was dated 1554.
If born in 1514 he was already forty at the time !
Surely that speaks for itself ? These and yet
other considerations caused Haberl to reconsider
his position, and in 1888 he wrote : * " Our eye-
witness (Melchior major †) has given trustworthy
proof of Palestrina's age and, consequently, for
the year of the Roman master's birth : *not* in 1514
but in 1526 is it my well-grounded conviction
that Palestrina was born."

This testimony was considered final, all subsequent writers following Haberl's lead. But a

* Haberl, F. X., *Bibliographischer und thematischer Musik-
katalog*. 1888.
† Haberl made a slip and wrote it Mafor instead of Major.

new pamphlet cuts the matter still finer.* There
it is pointed out that Melchior stated Pierluigi's
age on the day of his death to be sixty-eight.
In that case he *was* sixty-eight. If, then, his
birthday did not happen to fall in January he was
already sixty-eight in the year 1593, in which case
68 subtracted from 1594 left the date of his birth
1525, not 6. The difference, it is true, is not
great, but it is a practical emendation, so much
so that in future it will be necessary to give the
great Palestrinian's birth as "between the years
1525 and 1526."

In connection with this inquiry the following
curious story may not be without interest. It
was related to the present writer by a prominent
biographer and fellow-townsman of Pierluigi.
He discovered, during some research work, a
manuscript in a certain Augustinian monastery
which he considered, on a hasty inspection, to be
highly important ; in particular, bearing on the
burning question of Pierluigi's birth-date. As it
was very difficult to decipher, and as he was
unable at the moment to give it the attention it
undoubtedly deserved, he left it on that day, but
lost no time in writing to the monastery for permission to have the document photographed.
Unfortunately, between the request and the

* *Palestrina's Geburtsjahr.   Eine historisch-kritische Untersu-
chung von Karl Weinmann.   Regensburg und Rom.   1915.*

subsequent permission the manuscript had disappeared. Some one, following hard on this
student's heels, had likewise gauged the extreme
importance of the discovery, and, less scrupulous,
quietly put the MS. in his pocket without
troubling about the formality of asking. This
was in 1912, and it may be that the events which
filled the ensuing years are alone responsible for
the circumstance that the world is still in doubt—
or at least in conflict—as to the year of Pierluigi's
birth.

However this may be, the enormous output
achieved by the Master—were his life ten years
longer than Melchior Major has given posterity
reason to believe—would still remain amazing.
Ninety-three masses, two hundred and fifty-six
motets,* four books of madrigals, not counting
the hymns and offertories for the whole of the
Church year, the three books of Magnificats, the
same number of Litanies, of Lamentations ; two
books of *Madrigali Spirituali*, constitute a formidable list and prove Pierluigi to have been an
extraordinarily hard worker. Assuredly they
were not all on the same grand level of inspiration, how should they be ? which is, after all,
only another way of saying that Pierluigi was
human. Some of the compositions were " sur
commande," others contrapuntal *tours de force*.

* Including one or two doubtful or wrongly attributed.

Nevertheless, the number of masterpieces is marvellously high. Baini distinguishes—with more ingenuity than usefulness—eight styles or genres of composition in the Master's art which he proceeds to subdivide into yet others : for instance, a first epoch in which Pierluigi was not yet freed from his Netherlandish fetters ; a second while under the influence of Festa and the post-Josquin School ; a third dominated by Morales and the Spaniards. In the fourth Baini pronounces him to have found himself—and so on, and so forth. It may be questioned whether such arbitrary landmarks in the life of a great man serve any useful purpose. A more fruitful study would possibly be an inquiry into the different founts of expression—if the term be permitted—to which he went for his inspiration. As it was customary to compose the six sections of a mass on one theme, or different sections of one theme, it was a matter of extreme importance to find one that lent itself to a characteristic and suitable treatment. It has already been pointed out more than once in the foregoing pages what these themes usually were, and to a limited extent the choice determined the particular treatment accorded to the composition. Thus, if the theme were more or less secular in character it was often (though certainly not always) the occasion for a most elaborate contrapuntal exhibition in which

Pierluigi delighted to show his extraordinary mastery of the material. Instances of this are afforded by the masses *Ecce Sacerdos Magnus,* *L'homme armé,* and *Ad fugam.* Taken from a Gregorian melody it often received a devout, inspired yet ceremonial impress in keeping with its sacerdotal origin. In the masses of greater scope, such as *Ecce ego Joannes* or *Dum complerentur,* the invariable strength of phrase and intensity of expression are in direct contrast with some of the smaller though equally beautiful works, such as *Aeterna Christi munera, Iste Confessor,* and *Missa brevis,* in which the musical phrase is shorter, more defined, and simpler in design ; or such works as *Assumpta est Maria* and the motets on the Song of Solomon display a quality more emotional, more direct, more personal. If Pierluigi selected a theme with strong Church associations he did not need so much to consider the form in which he should work on the imagination of his hearers as to enrich the texture by the reiteration of chosen phrases treated canonically. Examine the mass *Iste Confessor,* constructed on the Vesper hymn of that name, and it will be seen that in the first section of fourteen bars * there are no less than seven entries of the initial phrase of the hymn ; in the

---

* The modern edition has been put into bars for the convenience of present-day musicians.

second, of fifteen bars, there are nine entries of the second phrase of the theme ; and in the third section of fourteen bars, there are eight entries of the third phrase of the theme. Thus, in a composition comprising forty-three bars, Pierluigi employs three sections of his theme no less than thirty-four times. This is certainly an instance of close weaving, and it might have been expected that the result would be a strained and stilted work as " cribbed, cabined, and confined " as some Byzantine Madonna of the late period when measurements restricted the artist's imagination within iron limits and forced him to conform. Yet the *Kyrie* flows with inimitable suavity from start to finish, nor does the ear detect the constant reiteration of a given phrase. The art—the wonderful art of it ! It is like some marvellous piece of needlework, of web-like pattern, gleaming with gold, silver, and soft colours, obeying the hidden law of the design, but presenting an indefinite yet gorgeous whole. The eye endeavours to distinguish the course of one thread, only to be deflected by another. It receives no exact impression, but the vague perception it conveys to the brain is of an agreeable harmonious whole, rising to sensations of acute pleasure. This simile, however, fails in one important aspect. No general perception of colour could affect the mind so powerfully as sound, or produce the same moral effect. Pierluigi's music penetrates the depths of the soul, and its selflessness widens the conception of things appertaining to the spirit. More, far more than a new formula of art, it was founded on antiquity and built up on international inspiration. It was the consecration of sound, or to recall S. Filippo's admirable phrase for the last time, the contemplation of celestial things by means of heavenly harmonies.

It may be that the years will see a return to the ideals of unaccompanied polyphony ; there are many beautiful secrets there for the finding.* But first it is necessary to train those ears to hear, which, like the eyes to see, are indispensable for the contemplation of all things, celestial or otherwise ; in other words, the inner vision.

* Such seem already to have inspired Hans Pfitzner since the above sentence was written, whose opera *Palestrina* is so described : " Ein Werk von so reiner Gesinnung und einem so erhabenen Ernste, der dem Idealismus seines Schöpfers das Opfer einer Selbstverleugnung ohne jeden Seitenblick auf die Güter dieser Welt auferlegt . . . wird nie die Huld der Masse finden," etc.

INDEX TO MASSES

NOTE.—The prefaces to each volume of masses by the editors of the Collected Edition, published by Breitkopf and Härtel, Dr. P. Wagner's *History of the Masses*, Ambros' *History of Music*, have been largely drawn upon for the analytical remarks to index.

MISSARUM CUM 4 ET 5 VOCIBUS, LIBER PRIMUS. Rome. *Valerio et Aloysio Dorico* 1554. Five subsequent editions. Vol. x. Collected Edition, is reprinted from that of 1591, containing two additional masses—*Pro defunctis* and *Sine nomine*. First edition dedicated to Julius III.

I. *Ecce sacerdos magnus.* 4 v. In mixolydian mode. Theme derived from Choral Antiphon in *Missa de Confessore Pontifice.* An example of highly complicated note measurements — *tempus imperfectum, prolatio perfecta,* etc., with instance of *Hemolia Minor* (*i.e.* emphasis changed from triple to duple rhythm ; other examples may be found in the motet *Dies sanctificatus,* and a particularly beautiful one in the exquisite motet *O magnuum mysterium* at *Collandantes Dominum*). This is a *cantus firmus* mass built on the ancient model ; the theme remaining independent of the other voices. Owing to the interpolation of non-liturgical words it became obsolete after the injunctions to that effect from the Council of Trent.—C. Ed. Vol. 10, p. 3

II. *O Regem coeli.* 4 v. Another mensural curiosity, the theme from double sources, a *responsorium* in use during the Christmas octave * and a motet by Andreas Silva ;† it is thus an instance of a *missa*

* Haberl. † P. Wagner.

parodia, a newer form much affected by Josquin and the writers of his time.—C. Ed. Vol. 10, 32.

III. *Virtute magna.* 4 v. In mixolydian. Also from a double source—a *Responsorium* in Easter week or a motet by Andrea de Salva—therefore to be classed as a *missa parodia.* It is composed in the same highly complicated manner, the *Osanna* being in *tempus magnus imperfec.* and *proportio tripla maj.* with a canon in the *Agnus Dei.*—C. Edit. Vol. 10, 55.

IV. *Gabriel Archangelus.* 4 v. In transposed dorian, theme from a motet by Verdelot.*—C. Ed. 10, 80.

V. *Ad coenam agni providi.* 5 v. Theme from Easter hymn originally with same title, now altered to *Ad regias agni dapes* through changes in the breviary. An interesting example of the employment of canon in all five voices, on fragment of subject treated freely. In the *Christe* the original theme is given out by the fourth voice in semibreves.—C. Ed. 10, 105.

VI. *Pro defunctis* (only included in 4th edit. 1591). 5 v. The only example of a mass for the dead from Pierluigi's pen. It consists of *Kyrie, Offertorium Sanctus* and *Agnus,* the remaining portions of the mass—*Introitus, Graduale, Tractus,* and *Communio*—being sung in plainsong. For this reason the *Kyrie* is in the hypolydian mode, the *Offertorium* in hypodorian, *Sanctus* and *Benedictus* in dorian, and *Agnus Dei* in hypomixolydian transposed.—C. Ed. 10, 138.

VII. *Sine nomine* (only included in 4th edit. 1591). 6 v. In transposed phrygian. So far the theme has not been traced, it is characteristic of plainsong forms by which it seems to have been inspired.—C. Ed. 10, 153.

MISSARUM . . . LIBER SEGUNDUS. Rome, 1567. Published by the successors of Dorici. This volume was dedicated to Philip II. of Spain. In complete edition, Vol. 11.

I. *De beata Virgine.* 4 v. Inspired by the liturgical

* Idem.

melodies usual on this festival, which Pierluigi employs in different designs, sometimes giving the theme to one voice as written, or cutting it up into points of imitation and dividing it between the parts, or turning it into the subject for a canon. It conforms in mode to the different melodies, *Kyrie* dorian, *Gloria* mixolydian, *Credo* hypophrygian, *Benedictus* and *Agnus Dei* transposed ionian.—C. Ed. 11, 1.

II. *Inviolata.* 4 v. Takes its title and theme from an official melody usually employed in Advent. In hypolydian or transposed hypoionian.—C. Ed. 11, 21.

III. *Sine nomine.* 4 v. In hypophrygian mode. Its theme has not yet been traced.—C. Ed. Vol. 11, 41.

IV. *Ad fugam.* 4 v. The title must not be understood in the modern sense. The evolution of contrapuntal art had not yet proceeded so far. It refers here to a type of composition after the manner of Josquin and may be recommended to the student as a valuable instance of "spade work" through which the heights of *Missa Papae Marcelli* and *Assumpta est Maria* were reached. In the original only the *Cantus* and *Bassus* exist. While the astonishing dexterity of the double canons must be admired, the limits in which Pierluigi has here chosen to work are too narrow for beauty.—C. Ed. 11, 57.

V. *Aspice Domine.* 5 v. Theme taken from the third *Responsorium* on the first Sunday in November.* In Dorian mode.—C. Ed. Vol. 11, 71.

VI. *Salvum me fac.* 5 v. Related in type to the 5th *Responsorium* for Matins on Palm Sunday * also bears some resemblance to a motet by Jachet.† Transposed dorian.—C. Ed. Vol. 11, 97.

VII. *Missa Papae Marcelli.* 6 v. Theme from plainsong. In mixolydian mode. This mass should be studied for the transparency and suavity of phrase ; for the new and surprising harmonic effects achieved by

* Haberl.　　　　　　　　† P. Wagner.

passing notes and without departing from the strict rule ; for the frequent use of the ancient device of " nota cambiata " (changing note) in the melisma. —C. Ed. Vol. 11, 128.

MISSARUM . . . LIBER TERTIUS. Published in 1570 by the same firm as the precedent volume and with a similar dedication. Four re-issues, that of 1599 without the Hexachord mass.

I. *Spem in alium.* 4 v. Based on 1st nocturn for 5th Sunday in September.* The theme suggested by a model of Jachet's.† In aeolian mode.—C. Ed. Vol. 12, 3.

II. *Primi toni.* 4. v. The theme has been traced to a madrigal entitled " Io mi son giovinetta "—supposed to be by Domenico Ferrabosco. This *missa parodia* affords an instance of a double canon in *subdiapente,* the answer following at the space of a semibreve, which constitutes a remarkable contrapuntal achievement. Transposed dorian.—C. Ed. Vol. 12, 26.

III. *Brevis.* 4 v. This beautiful mass is founded on one by Goudimel *Audi filia.* It is one of the best known to-day on account of its moderate length— many others, timed for the lengthy ceremonies in St. Peter's, proving quite unmanageable for ordinary occasions. It takes its title from the first note (breve) of the theme, and is in transposed ionian (XI).—C. Ed. Vol. 12, 50.

IV. *De Feria.* 4 v. In phrygian mode. Theme from plainsong takes its title from the days for which it is intended.—C. Ed. Vol. 12, 66.

V. *L'homme armé.* 5 v. In the mass *Ecce sacerdos magnus* an example of the finest shades of mensural combination and counterpoint were to be found ; but, considered from the point of view of artistic performance it would hardly be thought worth while to-day to prepare a hearing of this mass. *Ad fugam,* again, is to be regarded as a remarkable study in contrapuntal device, so closely knit that even Pierluigi's genius does not succeed in breaking out

* P. Wagner.   † Haberl,

into the free air of Heaven ; but in the " Omme
armé" (No. 1—there were two) is to be discerned
not only a "tour de force" so extraordinary that
even as late as 1592—and again in 1613, when
already this species of art was dead—Zacconi and
Cerone, the theorists of their time, give an analysis
of it—but a masterpiece which would certainly
make as profound an impression to-day as it did
many years ago when performed by a picked choir at
Regensburg. Though Pierluigi has here chosen the
older form of a *cantus firmus* mass, his procedure is
essentially modern (of his time) and he gives it new
life, enclosing the theme with a wealth of melodies,
proceeding with so much freedom in his treatment
of the parts, grouping his voices with so much contrast, that it would certainly never be suspected by
the uninitiated that each step was subject to an all-
controlling law and that the path was so narrow
which led to salvation. The mode is hypomixolydian. While the tenor sings in *Tempus perfectum
cum prolatione* the other voices are in *tempus perfectum
integri valor.* which, as has been remarked,* gives in
reality *tempus imperfectum.*—C. Ed. Vol. 12, 75.

VI. *Repleatur os meum laude.* 5 v. Of this mass it has been
said that " it breathes canons in every possible interval." † It opens with one in diapason. In the

first *Agnus Dei* the sign is to be taken

as indicating that the canon must be deciphered
with half-time note values.‡ Two sources are given
for this theme, a *responsorium* for Thursday in the
second week after Epiphany‡ and a motet by
Jachet.§ In phrygian mode.—C. Ed. Vol. 12, 105.

VII. *De beata Virgine vel Dominicalis.* 6 v. Once again
Pierluigi employs as theme the melodies set apart
for this festival. The tropes—*Mariam gubernans*—
Mariam coronans, or intercalation of non-liturgical

* Haberl.   † P. Wagner.
‡ Haberl.   § Wagner.

text, once customary but later abolished by the Council of Trent, were removed in the 1599 edition, and liturgical words inserted in their place. The *Kyrie, Gloria,* and *Credo* are respectively in the dorian, phrygian, and aeolian modes, etc.— C. Ed. Vol. 12, 135.

VIII. *Ut, re, mi, fa, sol, la.* 6 v. Or Hexachord mass. Pierluigi here follows the example of Brumel and others in taking as his theme the Guidonian Hexachord in two out of the three forms—*durum* and *naturale* (see Appendix); the *molle* is discarded on account of its modulating property (mi-fa or A-B♭). It is sung by *Cantus II.* as a *cantus firmus* and thus the mass forms a particularly interesting example of the older model combined with a sense of effect, of proportion and clearness, a foretaste of the perfection shortly to be reached in the Marcellus mass. It was copied into the choir-books of the Sixtine Chapel as early as 1562. The mode is ionian.— C. Ed. Vol. 12, 165.

MISSARUM . . . LIBER QUARTUS. Dedicated to Gregory XIII. and published by Angelo Gardano of Venice. The seven masses it contains are without distinctive titles. These were added to some extent in the collected editions as the themes were traced.

I. *Missa prima (Lauda Sion).* 4 v. The theme is taken from the sequence appertaining to the Festival of

Corpus Christi . In

Lau - da Si - on   Sal - va - tor - em

hypomixolydian.—C. Ed. Vol. 13, 1.

II. *Missa secunda (Primi toni).* 4 v. In transposed dorian. Theme hitherto not identified.—C. Ed. Vol. 13, 15.

III. *Missa tertia. (Jesu nostra redemptio.)* 4 v. From the Pentecostal hymn of that title.

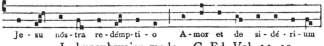

Je - su nós - tra re - démp - ti - o   A - mor et de si - dé - ri - um

In hypophrygian mode.—C. Ed. Vol. 13, 29.

IV. *Missa quarta.*   4 v.   Pierluigi's second mass over the celebrated theme of L'homme armé and the variation of treatment is highly interesting. As has recently been pointed out * the subject here is in the dorian, which, from our point of view, constitutes a minor key  with its minor 3rd. In the first mass, however, it is in the mixolydian mode ; or, again, from the modern theoretical standpoint is major—

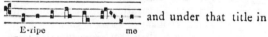

This obviously changes the whole character of the composition, and the contrast does not alone consist in this.   In mass No. 1 Pierluigi was, as it were, entering the lists to break a lance with some very redoubtable knights.   In short, his reputation was at stake.   In mass No 2, no such considerations were necessarily present, therefore the mass is shorter, less astonishing, on a later model and written in the style which he brought to such perfection, the voices moving throughout in perpetual imitation.— C. Ed. Vol. 13, 45.

V. *Missa prima (Eripe me de inimicis).*   5 v.   Taken from the verses for the 9th Sunday after Pentecost

and under that title in a Codex in the Vienna Court Library.   In dorian mode.—C. Ed. Vol. 13, 59.

VI. *Missa secunda.*   5 v.   Theme not traced.   Transposed dorian.—C. Ed. Vol. 13, 85.

VII. *Missa tertia.* (*O magnum mysterium.*)   5 v.   Taken from Pierluigi's beautiful motet of the same title, this theme—as those of Nos. I, III, and V,—serves to prove that the numbered mass did not necessarily conceal a secular origin.   The mode is hypophrygian.—C. Ed. Vol. 13, 110.

* P. Wagner.

Missarum . . Liber Quintus. Published in Rome by Coattino and dedicated to Duke William of Bavaria—the patron of Lassus—in 1590.

I. *Aeterna Christi munera.* 4 v. Theme taken from a hymn sung at Matins on Apostles' and Evangelists' days. It runs thus:

Ae - ter - na Chris - ti   mu - ne - ra

One of the best known of Pierluigi's shorter masses in modern times on account of its fresh well-contrasted part writing, moderate difficulty, and convenient length. The mode is transposed ionian.—C. Ed. Vol. 14, 1.

II. *Jam Christus astra ascenderat.* 4 v. Theme from Ascentiontide hymn. Transposed dorian.—C. Ed. Vol. 14, 15.

III. *Panis quem ego dabo.* 4 v. Two sources have been suggested for the theme of this mass—a motet by Johannes Lupus * and another by Jachet.† In hypodorian mode.—C. Ed. Vol. 14, 34.

IV. *Iste Confessor.* 4 v. This beautiful mass, another of the best known amongst the shorter masses, is founded on the Latin hymn of the same name. Indeed, one cannot help wondering whether Pierluigi was not indisposed to give Lassus a practical illustration, in dedicating this volume to Duke William of Bavaria, that a worthier source for his themes than that from which the great Netherlander frequently took them was at hand in music already dedicated to the Church. Mode hypodorian.—C. Ed. Vol. 14, 54.

V. *Nigra sum.* 5 v. This Missa Parodia is founded on Pierluigi's motet from the beautiful series—29 in number—on the Song of Solomon. The mode is transposed hypoaeolian.—C. Ed. Vol. 14, 66.

VI. *Sicut lilium.* 5 v. A similar source. In transposed aeolian.—C. Ed. Vol 14, 95.

* Haberl.   † P. Wagner.

VII. *Nasce la gioia mia.* 6 v. Theme from a madrigal
written by Gio. Leonardo Primavera dell' Arpa,
published in 1565.* Transposed Dorian.—C. Ed.
Vol. 14, 118.

A re-edition in the following year by Scoto of Venice contained the additional mass *Sine nomine* already mentioned as
included in the 1591 edition of *Liber Primus.* (See p. 193,
Index.)

LIBER SEXTUS . . . MISSAE QUINQUE 4 AC 5 VOCIBUS CON-
CINATUS. This volume, dedicated to Cardinal Pietro Aldobrandini, was published by Coattino of Rome in the year
1594. It appeared a month after Pierluigi's death.

   I. *Dies santificatus.* 4 v. The theme taken from Pierluigi's
motet in four parts (there were two—the second in
eight parts) with a similar title (Vol. 5 of Collected
Edit. p. 3). It is in the mixolydian mode. While
the opening is almost identical he works up his
thematic material, the result being much richer in
effect and thus forming a valuable example of the
master's methods. The hemolia minor should be
noted.—C. Ed. Vol. 15, 1.

   II. *In te Domine speravi.* 4 v. Apparently based on
Offertorium for the 1st Tuesday in Lent.† In
dorian mode.—C. Ed. Vol. 15, 22.

  III. *Sine nomine.* 4 v. The theme has been traced to a
mass composed by J. Maillard on his own theme
" Je suis deshéritée," which was published by the
Parisian firm Adrien le Roy and Robert Ballard in
1557.—C. Ed. Vol. 15, 44.

  IV. *Quam pulchra es.* 4 v. In Vol. 4 of C. Ed. is to be
found a motet with similar title in five parts but
different thematic material. The subject of the
mass in question has been traced ‡ to one by J.
Lupus on the same text (from the Song of
Solomon) in the Vienna Hofbibliothek. The
mode is ionian.—C. Ed. Vol. 15, 60.

  V. *Dilexi quoniam.* 5 v. Words taken from Ps. 114
(English Prayer-book 116). This mass, which

---

* P. Wagner.   † Haberl.   ‡ P. Wagner.

takes rank with Pierluigi's most inspired work, was
copied into the Papal Choir's book in the first year
of Sixtus V.'s reign (1585), and is still sung. It
is in the mixolydian mode.—C. Ed. Vol. 15, 84.
VI. *Ave Maria.* 6 v. This mass was only included
amongst the foregoing in the 2nd edition of this
volume, issued by Gardano of Venice in 1596. It
was probably sold by Igino to the Venetian publishers after his father's death.* As the Sextus

sings the C. F.

to the words *Ave Maria gratia plena* this circumstance justifies the identification of this mass as of
earlier origin.† It is written in a certain simple,
genial, pastoral vein, and it has therefore been suggested that it was intended for Christmastide. The
mode is transposed ionian.—C. Ed. Vol. 15, 113.

LIBER SEPTIMUS . . . MISSAE QUINQUE. 4 AC 5 VOCIBUS.
This volume, published in Rome by Coattino in 1594, was
hurried through the press immediately after Pierluigi's death
by his son Igino. It is probable that the Master had its contents already in contemplation, for the dedication bears the date
March 1, 1594. Igino, on hearing that His Holiness considered
a scheme for bringing out a complete edition of his late composer's works, dedicated this volume to Clemens VIII. The
record of the Pope's intention is made, as follows, by the
Puntatore to the Papal Choir—the occasion was the anniversary
of the Pope's coronation : "Di poi la messa si andi a cantar
li motteti al Papa mentre desinava, e di poi entrammo dentro
la stantia dove desinava. Et Sua Santità domandò a chi erano
restate le opere della bo · me · de Messer Giovanni di Pelestrino
(*sic*) Glie fu resposto che erano restate al figluolo ; et soggiunse
che voleva dar ordine che fussero di nuovo stampate e quello
anco, che non erano in luce, per utile delle chiese." ‡ It is
in Igino's dedication to Pope Clemens VIII. that he makes use
of those ambiguous terms which gave rise to so much con-

* Haberl.
† P. Wagner.
‡ Preface to Vol. 17, C. Ed.

troversy. *"Pater meus, septuaginta fere vitae suae annos in Dei laudibus componendis consumens."* * The 2nd edition in 1595 had an additional mass, *Ad beneplacitum,* included in *Liber Decimus* under the title *Illumina oculos meos,* the theme of which has been traced to a motet of the Papal singer Andrea de Silva.†

I. *Ave Maria.*   4 v.   Theme derived from 2nd Antiphon usual on the Festival of the Annunciation. Transposed dorian at the upper 5th. An interesting example of the manner in which Pierluigi works up a flowing but not particularly interesting subject, with an additional part (5 parts) in the second *Agnus.*—C. Ed. Vol. 16, 1.

II. *Sanctorum meritis.*   4 v.   Theme from the hymn *Sanctorum*

meritis

Sanc - to - rum me - ri - tis in - cly - ta gau - dia

etc. (see also Pierluigi's hymn, C. Ed. 8, p. 113). In phrygian mode. An example of Pierluigi's most suave and limpid part-writing, the *Crucifixus* and *Pleni sunt* in three parts and the contrasts marked between the higher and lower voices.—C. Ed. Vol. 16, 22.

III. *Emendemus.*   4 v.   Another mass in a similar vein. It has been suggested that the theme resembles that of *Sine nomine* in *Liber Sextus* (15th Vol. C. Ed.) ; but whether that be so or no (and there are certainly points of resemblance) Baini gives yet another derivation which it is, however, impossible to verify. He says it is founded on a motet by the Spaniard Gabriel Calvez, of which no trace can now be found. The mode is transposed hypodorian. —C. Ed. Vol. 16, 44.

IV. *Sacerdos et pontifex.*   5 v.   Derived from Magnificat Commune Conf. Pont. Mode II., transposed 4th above. With the other masses *Ascendo ad Patrem* and *Tu es Petrus* it was copied into the Sistine Chapel choir books in 1602. In hypodorian mode.—C. Ed. Vol. 16, 60.

* See page of G. P. da Pales., 183.   † P. Wagner.

V. *Tu es pastor ovium.* 5 v. Dedicated to Sixtus V. in the year of his accession. Taken from the 2nd part of motet with same title which itself is derived from the Gregorian melody of the Magnificat antiphon on the Festival of St. Peter (C. Ed. 31, 63). In dorian mode.—C. Ed. Vol. 16, 85.

(The new edition, 1595, contained an additional mass, *Ad bene placitum* or, as it appeared in a 1600 edition, "*Illumina oculos meos,*" printed in Vol. 19, p. 109, C. Ed.)

MISSARUM . . . LIBER OCTAVUS, 1599, published by Tiberius de Argentis and inscribed as follows :—
Admodum :

> *R.P.D. Sylvio Maioli Palavino Priori meritissimo P. Salvatoris in Lauro de Urbe ac Totius congregationis S. Georgii in Alga Procuratori Generali. D. Tiberius de Argentis foelicitatem Venetiis 1599 Die vigesima Mensis Aprilis.*

I. *Quem dicunt homines.* 4 v. Haberl totally disagrees with Baini's criticism of this as a youthful work, saying it belongs to a ripe period and is "fresh and living." In hypomixolydian mode. Dr. P. Wagner thinks it is derived from a motet by Jean Richafort.—C. Ed. Vol. 17, 1.

II. *Dum esset summus pontifex.* 4 v. Derived from Antiphon to Magnificat for 2nd Vesper in the *Commune sanctorum summorum pontificum.* In Dorian mode.— C. Ed. Vol. 17, 23.

III. *O admirable commercium.* 5 v. Inspired by his own motet (with similar title) which was derived from the first Vesper Antiphon for the Christmas octave. Written in mixolydian mode, it is a composition of peculiar loveliness.—C. Ed. Vol. 17, 39.

IV. *Memor esto.* 5 v. From motet with similar title.— C. Ed. Vol. 17, 63.

V. *Dum complerentur.* 6 v. From motet of same name. C. Ed. 1, 3. Copied into Codex 32 of Sistine Chapel in 1585. Full of the spirit of Whitsuntide. Transposed ionian.—C. Ed. Vol. 17, 85.

VI. *Sacerdotes Domini.* 6 v. Pierluigi has here taken the words of the Offertorium on the Festival of *Corpus Christi, Sacerdotes Domini incensum et panes offerunt*

Deo, etc., and with the memory of the Festival of the Trinity in his mind, has set himself to illustrate the mystery with a marvellous double canon, inscribed *Trinitas in unitate.* No mere example of pedantic learning, it is a triumphant statement of an article of faith. It is in the VIII. mode. Haberl remarks that the 8th Volume is one of the best and worthiest collections of masses written by the Master. The Editor, D. Tiberius de Argentis, sums them up : " *Divino furore afflatus vir recolendae memoriae Joann. Petraloysius Praenestinus hoc nostro sœcolo admirabilis in componendis cantibus pro uso Ecclesiae Catholicae has praesertim Missas composuit.*" Between 1599 and 1601, D. T. de Argentis edited the 8th, 9th, 11th, 12th, and 13th books of masses. In dedicating Vol. 8 to the Prior of the congregation, *S. Salvatoris in Lauro de Urbe* (Rome) and *S. Georgii in Alga* (Venice), it is not yet clear what his position was in regard to this congregation. It has been suggested that as the church S. Salvatore in Lauro (Rome) was frequented by the Papal Singers, in this way, D. T. de Argentis came into possession of Palestrina's masses (Haberl).—C. Ed. Vol. 17, 113.

MISSARUM . . . LIBER NONUS. This volume was brought out by D. T. de Argentis ten months after *Liber Octavus.* The date is Feb. 20, 1599, but owing to differences in the Venetian Calendar this should probably be altered to 1600. The description is as follows : *Cantus | Joannis. Petraloysis Praenestini | Missarum cum quatuor, quinque, et sex vocibus | LIBER NONUS | . . . Venetiis Apud Haeredem Hieronymi Scoti MDXCIX.* This volume also was dedicated to a member of the Congregation of S. Giorgio in Alga, Giovanni Cisani of Verona.

I. *Ave regina coelorum.* 4 v. Inspired by 1st Antiphon, B.M.V., and in the same mode (hypoionian). A mass of similar length to *Iste Confessor* and *Aeterna Christi munera.*—C. Ed. Vol. 18, 1.

II. *Veni sponsa Christi.* 4 v. Taken from his motet, based on the Gregorian melody *Veni Sponsa Christi*

(Antiphon to Mag. Commune Virginum).—C. Ed. Vol. 18, 21.

III. *Vestiva i colli.* 5 v. Taken from his madrigal of same name. It has also been suggested that it owes something to the *Sequence Victimae Paschali laudes*, as it is full of Easter joy. In dorian mode. —C. Ed. Vol. 18, 38.

IV. *Sine nomine.* 5 v. A marvel of contrapuntal dexterity. In the 1st *Kyrie* a canon in the upper fifth resolved after one half pause : in the *Christe* a canon in the upper fourth resolved after two half pauses. In the last *Kyrie* a canon in the octave resolved after three half pauses, in *Et in terra* canon in the lower second after four half pauses, in the *Qui tollis* canon in the upper second after five half pauses, in the *Patrem* canon in the upper third after six half pauses, *Et in spiritum* canon in the lower third after seven half pauses, *Sanctus* canon in the upper sixth after eight half pauses, *Hosanna* and *Benedictus* canon in the lower sixth after nine half pauses, first *Agnus Dei* in the lower seventh after ten, second *Agnus Dei* canon in the upper seventh after eleven half pauses. This *tour de force*, as was only to be expected, is not one of Pierluigi's most genial works. In dorian mode.—C. Ed. Vol. 18, 64.

V. *In te Domine, speravi.* 6 v. Baini rightly praises this mass for its clarity, strength, magnificence, its elegance of proportion, vocal qualities and spontaneity. It is certainly one of the most delightful compositions in the Master's suave and soaring manner. It appears to be based on the Gregorian melody of the Ambrosian hymn.* In the XI. (ionian mode).—C. Ed. Vol. 18, 91.

VI. *Te Deum laudamus.* 6 v. Like the plainsong melody from which it is derived, in Phrygian mode (two forms), copied into Codex 32 of Pap. Ch. with date 1585 at the same time as *Deus complerentur, Viri Galilei* and *Aspice Domine.* The mode gives the mass a certain severity of colouring but is full of holy fire.†--C. Ed. Vol. 18, 119.

* Haberl.   † Idem.

MISSARUM . . . LIBER DECIMUS. This was published in 1600 by Andreas de Agnetis, also a Venetian, of whom nothing is known. He bought the masses from Igino. The original title of the volume runs : *Cantus | Joan | Petraloysii | Praenestinus Missarum cum quatuor, quinque, et sex vocibus | LIBER DECI-MUS | . . .* Venetiis *Apud Haeredem Hieronymi Scoti M.D.C.*

I. *In illo tempore.* 4 v. Probably an early work derived from motet of same title. In dorian (I.) mode. Only one *Agnus Dei,* in canon at the upper fourth. Haberl considered it an uneven and unpractical mass.—C. Ed. Vol. 19, 1.

II. *Già fu chi m'ebbe cara.* 4 v. Taken from the madrigal in 28th Vol. C. Ed., p. 26, published in 1555. Baini says : "*à breve armoniosa, ben misurata nei periodi, leggiera, e vivacetta.*" An unusual feature is the double canon in the *Benedictus.* This mass is to be found in a Folio Codex 1692, from the Hospital of *S. Spirito in Sassia, Roma,* with the title "Jam fuit," and the author is given as *Palestina Praenestinae !* C. Ed. Vol. 19, 22.

III. *Petra Sancta.* 5 v. Theme untraced. In aeolian mode. Baini's criticism is "severe and weighty."— C. Ed. Vol. 19, 37.

IV. *O Virgo simul et mater.* 5 v. Based on the motet with similar title (C. Ed. 2, 3) published in 1572. Haberl draws attention to the first bar, p. 79, between 1st alto and tenor, where are to be found examples of fifths "which are no printer's error."— C. Ed. Vol. 19, 63.

V. *Quinti toni.* 6 v. This mass, ostensibly in the lydian mode, is, in Haberl's opinion, so-called by the editor Agnetis on finding it without a title, for, according to Venetian custom, the lydian was treated as the ionian mode, *i.e.* with the flat fourth. As this was not Pierluigi's custom it would be a matter for astonishment had he departed from it here. Baini says of this mass "*è bellissima, d'un effetto mirabile, ricercatissima nella modulazione, e si debbe avere per una delle più solenni e sublimi messe che uscissero della penna di Giovanni.*"—C. Ed. Vol. 19, 85.

VI. *Illumina oculos meos.* 6 v. A particularly earnest and devotional mass, too much so, indeed, for Baini's Latin taste, which assigns it to the "scuola fiamminga." It is, nevertheless, one of the composer's masterpieces. Taken from a motet by A. de Silva this mass was already included in the second (1595) edition of *Liber Septimus* under the title of *Ad bene placitum.*—C. Ed. Vol. 19, 109.

MISSARUM . . . LIBER UNDECIMUS was issued by Girolamo Scoto of Venice and dedicated by the editor, Tiberius de Argentis, to the Prior, Daniel Rosa, of the Congregation of S. Gregorius in Alga with S. Gregorio and S. Vitale. The full title is as follows : *Cantus | Joannis Petraloysii | Praenestini | Missarum cum quator, quinque et sex vocibus : | Liber Undecimus | . . . Venetiis, Apud Haeredem Hieronymi Scoti M.D.C. |* Date of dedication November 10, *1600.*

I. *Descendit Angelus Domini.* 4 v. Derived from a motet by Hilaire Penet.* In ionian mode, translated in the upper 4th with a ♭. Simple, clear, and agreeable though somewhat spun-out.† The illustration of the text in the *Gloria* should be noted where the *Cantus* touches G on the word *altissimus* for the only time throughout this section, also the joyous sequential passages in the opening of the *Credo.*—C. Ed. Vol. 20, 1.

II. *Regina coeli.* 5 v. This joyous mass in the same mode as the preceding derives its subject from the Antiphon proper to Easter, a fresh development of which is easily traced in the *Christe.* The *Hosanna in excelsis* is a pæan of transcendent joy, the effect of which is in some measure due to the change of rhythm, the time signature being $\frac{3}{1}$.—C. Ed. Vol. 20, p. 22.

III. *Quando lieta sperai.* 5 v. Dr. Wagner has traced this subject to a madrigal by Cyprian de Rore. The mass is in the aeolian mode. A copy without the title is to be found in Cambridge in the Fitzwilliam Museum.—C. Ed. Vol. 20, p. 50.

* P. Wagner.   † Haberl.

IV. *Octavi toni.* 6 v. This mass, in the hypomixolydian mode, is interesting on account of its tonality, much in advance of the period. It might almost, indeed, have been considered from an early harmonic standpoint. A *cantus firmus* allied in character to that employed in *Ecce sacerdos magnus* runs through the 2nd soprano voice-part of the *Kyrie, Sanctus,* and *Benedictus* in breves, adapted to triple measure in the final *Agnus Dei.*—C. Ed. Vol. 20, p. 80.

V. *Alma Redemptoris.* 6. v. This beautiful mass, in transposed ionian, is another instance of Pierluigi's exaltation in connection with the Mother of God. Founded on the antiphon usual in the Advent season it is written in a spirit of intense devotion and holy joy. The 6-part hosanna in triple measure, divided between the higher and lower voices for the first ten bars, is especially remarkable. —C. Ed. Vol. 20, p. 106.

MISSARUM . . . LIBER XII. was dedicated by Tiberius de Argentis to another of the canons of S. Giorgio in Alga, the Vicar, J. B. Bordone, the contents, with one exception, hitherto unpublished. It was issued by Scoto of Venice and dated April, 1601.

I. *Regina cœli.* 4 v. This mass (in transposed hypo-ionian mode) though founded on the same theme as the 5-part mass published on p. 22 of Vol. 20, C. Ed., is treated differently, for that reason forming an interesting comparison.—C. Ed. Vol. 21, 1.

II. *O Rex gloriae.* 4 v. The master's motet (5th Vol. C. Ed. p. 26) formed the basis of this mass in transposed hypodorian. Not alone the influence of the tonality, but the awe and veneration inspired by the season (Ascensiontide) accounts for the deeply solemn spirit in which this mass is composed. Possibly an early work. In the *Benedictus* and *Agnus Dei* are to be found examples of a canon in unison.—C. Ed. Vol. 21, p. 22.

III. *Ascendo ad Patrem.* 5 v. Another Ascensiontide mass, but here the joy of the wonderful event outweighs

P

the awe. It opens with the rise of an octave, imitated in all the parts ; a naïve illustration of the title. Haberl describes this mass as a costly pearl, and the student is unlikely to challenge this appreciation. The Sanctus especially, conveying the sense of soaring rapture, and the cumulating Hosanna (in which there is a change to triple measurement and a *Falso-bordone* effect, expressive in its simplicity) cannot fail to make a deep impression on the hearer.—C. Ed. Vol. 21, p. 38.

IV. *Qual è il più grand 'amor.* 5 v. Dr. Wagner finds some resemblance in the theme to a madrigal by Cyprian de Rore. In any case its origin is probably from some such source. It is in the hypoionian mode (transposed).—C. Ed. Vol. 21, p. 62.

V. *Tu es Petrus.* 6 v. This fine mass (in the mixolydian mode) is founded on the 5th Antiphon at Vespers on the Feast of S. Peter and Paul. It was copied as late as 1612 into the choir books of the Papal Chapel with *Sacerdos et Pontifex* and *Ascendo ad Patrem.* A second mass with this title, equally in mixolydian mode, is to be found in Vol. 24, C. Ed. —C. Ed. Vol. 21, p. 86.

VI. *Viri Galilaei.* 6 v. Pierluigi's motet with similar title is the source of this mass in the dorian mode (transposed a 4th higher). From the character of the mode it is not so jubilant as other Ascensiontide masses, though a beautiful work enough ; indeed Baini says "*sublimemente bella.*"—C. Ed. Vol. 21, p. 111.

MISSARUM . . . LIBER XIII. (Vol. 22 of the C. Ed.) appeared 20 days only after Vol. 12. Published by Amadino of Venice, it was the last issued by Tiberius de Argentis, dedicated to the Father General of the canons of St. George. Tiberius in this dedication compares Pierluigi to the sun amongst the stars (*Sol inter sidera*), which shows that the great composer's reputation had not waned in the intervening seven years since his death, and suggests that the 8-part masses contained in the present volume are amongst his most celebrated works. In Venice these would naturally meet with particular success, where the broad effect of contrasting choirs was much developed. At the same time there is more subtlety in the parts where the number of voices is confined to five or six, the interweaving receiving no aid from mere "effectiveness," but depending on solid counterpoint. The first three masses of this series were unpublished before this date (1601); the fourth appeared in Pierluigi's lifetime.

I. *Laudate Dominum omnes gentes.* 8 v. On Pierluigi's motet of same title. The *Christe* is sung alone by the first choir. A similar contrast is obtained in the *Crucifixus.* The mode is transposed dorian.— C. Ed. Vol. 22, p. 1.

II. *Hodie Christus natus est.* 8 v. The delightful and well-known Christmas motet with similar title is the basis of this mass. The effective change of rhythm in the motet to the words *no-e, no-e,* is transformed in the mass to *Hosanna in excelsis* following the *Benedictus.* Here the two choirs are contrasted in quality, the first consisting of high, the second of lower voices, giving a very rich effect. The mode is mixolydian.—C. Ed. Vol. 22, p. 40.

III. *Fratres ego enim accepi* (double choir). 8 v. From the 8-part motet of similar title. In transposed dorian. Haberl points out a passage in *Agnus Dei* between the altos of the first and second choirs with octaves, which Baini later corrected.—C. Ed. Vol. 22, p. 74.

IV. *Confitebor tibi Domine* (double choir). 8 v. From a similar source and in same mode. It was published in 1585. Written in a reflective, earnest style it displays certain beautiful effects, such, for instance, as the opening bars of the 2nd choir (*cantus* and *altus*) on the high G and its octave.—C. Ed. Vol. 22, p. 110.

Volume 23 of the C. Ed. contains six hitherto unpublished masses, which were put into score from MSS. in the Vatican or Sixtine Chapel libraries. Baini had already made copies, which were checked with the original MSS. and used in the collected edition.

I. *In majoribus duplicibus.* 4 v. Pierluigi took the

customary Gregorian melodies for this class of festival, either in the original mode or transposing them a fourth higher. Thus, the *Kyrie* is in the phrygian, the *Gloria* in the mixolydian, the *Sanctus* and *Benedictus* in transposed dorian (upper 4th), and the *Agnus Dei* ionian.—C. Ed. Vol. 23, p. 1.

II. *In minoribus duplicibus.* 4 v. Of similar origin. The fundamental melodies are to be found under the heading *in festis duplicibus* in the so-called *Ordinarium missae.* Pierluigi has transposed the modes (originally dorian and phrygian) in the upper 4th, *Credo* dorian, *Sanctus* and *Benedictus* mixolydian (transposed upper 4th), *Agnus Dei* lydian (transposed upper 5th).—C. Ed. Vol. 23, 26.

III. *Beatus Laurentius.* 5 v. Pierluigi wrote two motets with this title. The present mass is inspired by that one published in C. Ed. Vol. 1, 61, based on 5th Vesper Antiphon for August 10 (St. Lawrence). The mode is transposed hypomixolydian. Baini distinguishes the maturity of style in the mass from the motet written earlier.—C. Ed. Vol. 23, 48.

IV. *O sacrum convivium.* 5 v. A similar source. In ionian mode. This masterpiece was copied into the choir-books in 1594 (Codex 30).—C. Ed. Vol. 23, 71.

V. *Assumpta est Maria.* 6 v. In spite of the anecdotes Baini relates in connection with this mass, Haberl is of opinion it was not published before the year 1612 to 1630. Ambros considers it to belong to that group of masterpieces such as the Marcellus mass, the *Stabat Mater,* and the Song of Solomon motets. It is in the mixolydian mode.—C. Ed. Vol. 23, 97.

VI. *Veni Creator spiritus.* 6 v. This mass was copied into Codex 57, possibly in 1571, without a title, but the Pentecostal hymn forms the groundwork of the entire mass. In mixolydian mode.—C. Ed. Vol. 23, 122.

The final volume of masses, No. 24 in the C. Ed., contains none published before the nineteenth century.

I. *Pater noster.* 4 v. Pierluigi's motet, published in 1575, was founded upon the Gregorian melody associated with these words, around which he weaves his rich counterpoint. The mass is on similar lines and in hypodorian mode.—C. Ed. Vol. 24, 1.

II. *Panem nostrum.* 5 x. From the same source and mode.—C. Ed. Vol. 24, 20.

III. *Salve regina.* 5 v. From the Antiphon *Salve regina*, but, as Haberl remarks, not used as *cantus firmus* but as a leading motive, fully stated in the *Kyrie*, *Sanctus*, and *Benedictus*.—C. Ed. Vol. 24, 46.

IV. *Sine titulo.* 6 v. It has been suggested that this mass is derived from a mass of Orlando di Lasso's (Haberl), or a motet of Josquin des Près (Wagner), entitled *Benedicta*. Be that as it may, its broad and suave style is in the most characteristic manner of the master. It is in the hypomixolydian mode.—C. Ed. vol. 24, 72.

V. *Tu es Petrus.* 6 v. The second mass with this title derived from second half of the motet of same name, *Quodcumque ligaveris*. In mixolydian mode.—C. Ed. vol. 24, 105.

VI. *Ecce ego Joannes,* 6 v. The long list of masses closes with one of the most inspired compositions of the Master. The beautiful words from the liturgy on the Feast of All Saints receive fitting illustration, and there is true prophetic dignity and authority in a work some would even place at the head of all others.—C. Ed. Vol. 24, 129.

APPENDIX

SIXTEENTH CENTURY ART

THE theory on which the works of the great Roman School were constructed was third in the order of succession, and took shape somewhere between the appearance of Johannes Tinctoris' *Expositio Manus,* about 1470, and Pietro Aron's *De harmonica institutione,* in 1516 : its predecessors being the neumes, and the solmisation or mutation, system. The first-named was a method of demonstrating direction but not duration or pitch ; the second, beginning with a fixed point of departure—the first line of a stave standing for the bass F—developed into a scale of twenty notes, the five-lined stave, and a system of modulation within those limits by means of a movable hexachord which, under the successive names of *hexachordum durum, hexachordum naturale,* and *hexachordum molle* covered the whole of the constituted scale. But there were certain difficulties, and in resolving these the theorists paved the way to very radical changes indeed. Up to this point the whole structure of music rested on the foundation of ancient modes or scales in which the Church melodies were written. Any change in these was regarded as little short of sacrilege, and when this was found to be unavoidable, musicians invented the formula of *musica ficta,* a way of correcting the obnoxious interval of a tritone or augmented fourth—known throughout the Middle Ages as a *diabolus in musica*—by means of a flat. Though the application of the principle was new, a similar idea is to be found in the transpositional scales of the Greeks, from which the device of bridging the hexachords by a series of tetrachords

was also probably taken. The Guidonian * system was
constituted as follows :—

```
ee  . . . . . . . . . .   la ⎫
dd  . . . . . . . . . la ⎞ sol ⎮
cc  . . . . . . . . sol ⎮ fa  ⎮
bb  . . . . . . . . fa  ⎰ mi  ⎬
aa  . . . . . . . la ⎞ mi ⎛ re  ⎮
g   . . . . . . sol ⎮ re ⎮ ut  ⎭ Hexachordum durum superacutum.
f   . . . . . . . fa ⎰ ut ⎭ .   Hexachordum molle acutum.
e   . . . . . la ⎞ mi
d   . . . . la ⎞ mi ⎛ re
c   . . . sol ⎮ fa ⎮ ut ⎭ . . . Hexachordum naturale acutum.
b   . . . fa  ⎰ mi
a   . . la ⎞ mi ⎛ re
G   . sol ⎮ re ⎮ ut ⎭ . . . . . Hexachordum durum acutum.
F   . fa  ⎰ ut ⎭ . . . . . . Hexachordum molle grave.
E   la ⎞ mi
D   sol ⎮ re
C   fa  ⎰ ut ⎭ . . . . . . . Hexachordum naturale grave.
B   mi
A   re
Γ   ut ⎭ . . . . . . . . . . Hexachordum durum grave.
```

N.B.—The *Hexachordum molle* in every case is founded
on a *b rotundum*.†

And it will readily be seen that each of the tetrachords
had the semitone, or *mi-fa*, in a similar place ; that in the
case of the *hexachordum molle* it was necessary, in order to
bring this about, to employ a *b rotundum* instead of a
b durum,‡ a change too drastic to be acknowledged, but
left to the singer who recognized the necessity by the
rules supplied him. This theory of the hexachord was
never superseded, it became incorporated in its successor ;
just, indeed, as the neumes supplied the models from
which sixteenth-century notation arose, and this homoge-

* Guidonian, from Guido d'Arezzo, who either adapted or
invented the mutation system in the second quarter of the eleventh
century.

† Quoted by Ambros, *Geschichte der Musik*, vol. ii. p. 190.

‡ *b rotundum* = B♭ ; *b durum* or *quadrum* = B♮.

neity is a direct consequence of the veneration in which the ancient melodies were held, although the enormous developments which took place in the interval bore little resemblance to the primitive methods of early composers. Josquin was the first musician bold enough to break tradition so far as to insert a *b rotundum* where otherwise the employment might remain a matter of uncertainty ; but this innovation was resented by the singers, who, themselves mostly composers, regarded the signs as insults to their capacity. They went so far as to call them *asininos* (little asses). Nevertheless, it was obviously impossible—as music grew in subtlety—to trust to the intelligence of the choirs, and *asininos* had come to stay. Even so, composers used them as little as possible, and there is many a passage in the works of Pierluigi and his followers which present to the modern musician considerable difficulty of elucidation. Help may be sought in the contemporary theoretical works, though, unfortunately, they do not always agree.

The wonderful growth in musical theory during the fifteenth century was due not to the theorists, but to the composers, the extraordinary vitality of whose ideas is an astonishing feature of this period. The treatise writers followed, not led ; explaining, criticizing, condemning, or praising. Josquin's art was the crown of this great period, and his gift to the coming generation was a new freedom of which they were not slow to take advantage.

The Modes

At the beginning of the sixteenth century these stood thus constituted : there were six authentic scales and six plagal or derivative scales, the latter bearing a certain amount of analogy to a minor modern scale, with fundamental differences. In each and all of these the position of the semitone constituted the peculiar feature or characteristic of the mode.

The list and order is as follows :—

AUTHENTIC—	Dorian . . .	D E͡F G A B͡C D
	Phrygian . .	E͡F G A B͡C D E
	Lydian . . .	F G A B͡C D E͡F
	Mixolydian .	G A B͡C D E͡F G
	Aeolian . . .	A B͡C D E͡F G A
	Ionian . . .	C D E͡F G A B͡C
PLAGAL—	Hypodorian .	A b͡c D e͡f g a
	Hypophrygian.	B͡c d E͡f g a b
	Hypolydian .	C d e͡F g a b͡c
	Hypomixolyian	D e͡f G a b͡c d
	Hypoaeolian .	E͡f g A b͡c d e
	Hypoionian .	G a b͡C d e͡f g

(In the foregoing scales the semitones are marked as they occur and, in the case of the plagal scales, the finals are indicated by the second majuscule.) It will thus readily be seen that the authentic and its plagal (bearing the prefix *hypo*) possessed a common final or point of repose. In every composition the *cantus firmus* or tenor was required to finish on the final of the mode. At first sight it would seem impossible to ascertain whether the work was composed in an authentic or plagal mode. This question is only to be answered by an examination of the compass of the scale. Generally speaking, in the case of an authentic mode the melody did not proceed lower than a second below the final. On the other hand, the plagal scale might ascend one note higher than its octave and, in the case of the hypolydian and hypomixolydian modes, might descend to a fifth below its final. If, however, the course of the melody ran between the extreme points of a plagal *and* an authentic mode it was classified as *mixed.* There was yet one other distinction between an authentic mode and its plagal. This consisted in the natural division of the scale. The authentic mode was made up as follows :—

Dorian |D E F G A| (5th) |A B C D| (4th).

The plagal, on the contrary, was made up as follows :—

Hypodor. |A b c D| (4th) |D e f g a| (5th),

and this division served to mark the difference between an authentic scale and a plagal beginning on the same note.

Ex. Dorian . . |D E F G A̅ B C D̅.

Hypomixolydian |D e f G̅ a b c d̅.

In the case of a composition written in the dorian the dominant (A) would play an important part; were the composition, however, written in the hypomixolydian A would be of less importance, being the sixth of the mode, the final being G. It is only possible here to give a general idea of a highly complicated subject. *Each* of the modes, whether authentic or plagal, had its particular characteristics, which, if all were given here might only serve to confuse the reader. One word, perhaps, should be added with regard to the break in the order of the modes as shown above. This occurs between the aeolian and ionian authentic scales and their respective plagals, caused by the rejection of the intervening scales on account of the tritone and its inversion the diminished fifth. If it be inquired why the lydian (the first four notes of which constitutes an augmented fourth) and its plagal (with the inversion thereof) were allowed and not the Locrian (as it was called) and its *hypo*, the answer lies in the natural division of the scale :—

Lydian F G A B C̅ D E F

Locrian B C D E F̅ G A B

by which it is demonstrated that the essence of the
Locrian was a diminished fifth and tritone, a very *diabolus*
of a scale indeed !

MODULATION

In order to accommodate the voices of the singers it
might become necessary to change the compass of the
mode. This could not be done at will but within certain
arbitrary limits. A mode might be translated a fourth
above or a fifth below : or, a rare exception, a fifth above
and a fourth below. It is obvious that in performing this
operation the sequence of the tones and semitones had to
be preserved or the mode lost its individuality. But, if the
dorian (for example) be transposed a fourth higher the
natural disposition will either be changed, or the dorian
order must be created artificially :

$$\text{Dorian D } \hat{\text{E}} \text{ F G } \hat{\text{A}} \text{ } \hat{\text{B}}\text{C } \dot{\text{D}}$$

$$\text{Transposed Dorian G A } \ddot{\text{B}}\flat \text{ C } \dot{\text{D}} \text{ } \hat{\text{E}}\text{F } \dot{\text{G}}$$

Here came in the *b rotundum*, and by the sixteenth century
it took its place openly at the beginning of the stave,
signifying that the mode was a transposed one. But in
the case of a momentary modulation to another mode
where a *b rotundum* was necessary it either appeared at the
side of the note affected, or did *not* but was *musica ficta*
and supplied by the singer. In the treatises are to be
found examples of the rarely used inversion at the fifth
above; this process necessitated a sharp called a *diesis* in the
form of a St. Andrew's cross, otherwise this form was little
used, a *b durum* often being substituted for it. In con-
sidering these and similar points it is absolutely necessary
to dismiss from the memory all modern theories of key-
signatures. The employment of one flat does *not* constitute the key of F major, the employment of one sharp
the key of G major, which perhaps, after all, the reader
has already discovered for himself.

Other examples :—

Mixolydian G A B̂C Ḋ Ê F Ĝ,

trans. C D Ê F Ġ A ̂B♭ Ċ.

Phrygian Ê F G A B̂C D Ė,

trans. Â B♭ C D Ê F G Ȧ.

CLEFS

These comprised the different forms of the C, F, and G clefs, though towards the middle of the sixteenth century the G clef on the first line of the stave and the C on the last went out of general use. Though those most employed were the four used in ordinary score the choice was determined by the range of the melody, an important rule being that no voice-part should overflow the limits of the five-lined stave, its strictness being gauged by the scarce instances to the contrary. Thus, if the composition was in four parts, each voice had practically the choice of three clefs, the *cantus* or soprano being written in the two forms of the G, or the soprano C clef, the *altus* in the three forms of the C, soprano, mezzo-soprano, or alto; *tenor* in the alto, tenor or contra-tenor ; and the *bassus* in the three forms of the F clef, to which, indeed, might be added the two lowest forms of the C. Thus, if the student wishes to study the original scores for himself, without which it is impossible to form a true idea of polyphonic art, it is essential to master the use of the clefs.

TIME SYSTEM

This was very complicated, admitting a duple, triple, or triple *and* duple subdivision of the note according to position. As there were no bar-lines—limiting the difficulty of the problem to a small section of the stave—

there was no object in arranging the parts in score. Usually the voice-parts were contained in separate volumes; in the case of the great Roman editions and some others, the voices might be grouped two on a page, each, however, for itself, bearing no relation to the other. Thus, a continuous calculation on the part of the singer was necessary which, in the present day, has amusing and inconvenient results, for, in deciphering old scores, the misreading of a sign has not infrequently resulted in pages of cacophony and an appreciation of the unfortunate composer as primitive and barbarous! Thanks to the splendid labours of the editors of the collected edition Palestrina escaped this fate, but the added bar-lines have destroyed the appearance of the parts and *imitation* becomes harder to detect when the notes, to suit the exigencies of modern notation, are cut up into smaller values and slurred. Sixteenth-century time-signatures tended towards simplification if compared with those of the preceding century, but in order to appreciate this fact and to acquire a general idea of the system, it may be as well to give the table of note values, even though some of them were already out of use. The notes were grouped under three headings, Mode, Time, and Prolation. The mere choice of these terms is misleading to the modern student, the word Mode *not* here signifying the scale, the word Time *not* referring to all forms of rhythm. Therefore he must begin by disassociating these words from their accepted meaning and accept them at their sixteenth-century valuation.

Mode referred to the longest values of notes and their immediate subdivision.* It was susceptible of a double classification, *modus major perfectus* or the greater mode perfect, and *modus minor perfectus* or the lesser mode perfect, this subdivision again holding good in the case of *modus imperfectus*. Without spending much time on

---

* The Large and the Long only appear in sixteenth-century music to mark a long-held note at the close of a composition.

what was already obsolete by the middle of the sixteenth
century, it may be pointed out that perfect signified a
triple subdivision, imperfect a duple : that *modus major*
referred to the Large and its next smaller value, *modus
minor* to the Long and its next smaller value. The
modus major, perfect and imperfect, had these signatures :

Perf.   Imperf.

, and the *modus minor*, perfect and im-

perfect, these : Perf.   Imperf.   . The difficulty is increased

by the want of uniformity in the use of time-signatures,
but a circle always indicated perfect or triple time unless
accompanied by the figure 2, the half-circle imperfect or
duple time unless accompanied by the figure 3. The
next species is Time, referring to the breve and its next
value.   Again of two kinds, its signatures were as
follows :   Perfect.   Imperfect.   Prola-

tion concerned the semibreve and its next value—defined
as major and minor—on a similar principle, and by
Pierluigi's time it was again susceptible of a further duple
division into the semi-minima or chroma, where the rami-
fications of rhythm ended.* So far it was simple enough,
though a composition might require two or three signatures
to express, for example, *modus major perfectus, tempus imperfectus* and *prolatio minor*, which is to say that at one and
the same time the Large had a triple division, the Breve
a duple, and the Semibreve a duple, sufficiently puzzling
to a modern intelligence.† But the matter was complicated by black notes, which lost a fourth of their value

* Signatures of prolation :   Greater.   Lesser.

† The duration of these notes is not to be gauged by modern
estimates of *tempo*.

through their colour, by points of perfection, or of alteration, varying the usual procedure. These things require much study and experience, as also the ligatures, from which our slurred note, sung to one syllable, are descended. The account of these here would only serve to confuse the reader, for the different groups are very subtle and varied. The best way to approach their study is to take a good modern edition and compare it with the original. The following specimen may serve to illustrate these remarks and form a point of departure for future study.*

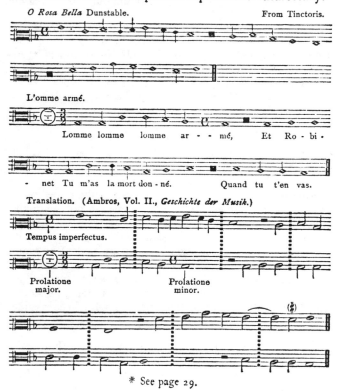

O Rosa Bella Dunstable.   From Tinctoris.

L'omme armé.

Lomme lomme   lomme   ar - - mé,   Et Ro - bi -

- net Tu m'as la mort don - né.   Quand tu t'en vas.

Translation. (Ambros, Vol. II., *Geschichte der Musik.*)

Tempus imperfectus.

Prolatione major.   Prolatione minor.

* See page 29.

CHARACTERISTICS OF THE ROMAN SCHOOL

While it must never be forgotten that the Roman school owed its theoretical development to an internationalism which reached its highest point in the Netherlands, it displayed from the first certain qualities more or less indigenous. These may be summed up as a stronger feeling for lucidity, taste, and proportion ; yet it is worth noting that, to some extent, the general trend of the sixteenth century elsewhere was in this direction.* Be this as it may, the best way to approach the study of the great polyphonic works of the Roman masters is surely through those of an earlier period, when it will be seen that the Southerners quickly distinguished themselves by a golden suavity partaking in its very essence of the environment in which they lived and worked. At the same time all the devices of the learned Netherlanders writing in the latter half of the fifteenth century are to be found in the compositions of the sixteenth in Italy, and there is abundant evidence that Pierluigi himself, while conscious of the direction in which his genius was leading him, was by no means inclined to forego the reputation of being even so learned a practitioner of his art as any of his Northern predecessors.

As a mature instance of this statement his Hexachord mass may be quoted, showing the fusion of old and new ideals. Written somewhere betweed 1561 and 1562— the date of its dedication to Pius IV. is 1562—it displays the characteristic clarity of phrase combined with a rich contrapuntal texture, with the most ingenious employment of its simple and at first sight uninteresting subject,

---

* The compositions of the little-known Clemens non Papa (of whom it is gravely asserted that he owed his curious name to the necessity of distinguishing him from the reigning Pontiff Clemens VIII.) furnish remarkable instances of this statement.

teeming with instances of *tempus perfectus,* close, even continuous, imitation and examples of *hexachordum naturale and durum* ; * with a *canon in sub diapente,* inversion of the *cantus firmus,* etc., etc. Notwithstanding this overwhelming display of erudition, it remains light and flowing, successfully concealing its prowess from the uninitiated. The *Crucifixus* is one of the most striking examples of the " Palestrinian " style the master ever penned, and announces his approaching zenith. It was indeed written to all appearances immediately before the Marcellus mass. Many of his shorter compositions are elaborate examples of the most complicated counterpoint from start to finish, as— for example—a passage in one of his *magnificats* where one tenor sings his part to its reversal in a second tenor part ! One of his favourite devices was to repeat a short phase at measured intervals, each time one degree of the scale higher, and in his *Missa sine nomine,* in the eighth volume of the complete edition, there are instances of double canons at the second and third which are a marvel of dexterity. Some of his most beautiful and characteristic effects, however, are also entirely simple. A case in point is his treatment of the fifth, which constituted a favourite opening chord. This venerable interval, along with the fourth and octave, was revered by the Greeks and revelled in by mediaeval musicians to the extent of whole compositions.† Tinctoris recommends it as an opening chord—with what propriety may be ascertained in the works of the great Palestrinian. Pierluigi's usual method of procedure is to sound one or other of the requisite notes alone, completing the chord on the entry of the second voice. Its acoustic perfection explains the peculiar satisfaction with which the ear receives it, and no doubt the large open spaces with lofty roofs in which these works

---

* Not *molle,* which would have led to difficulties of tonality.

† The late learned Belgian musician and critic, F. A. Gevaert, defended the cause of the fifth in parallel voices vigorously, claiming that although without an accompanying third the effect was characteristic and not inartistic.

are usually performed are for something in the sense of delight aroused in the hearer. It was this apparent simplicity of effect which constituted the great beauty of these *a cappella* works. It is, indeed, a curious fact that the complication of rhythm, so extreme, was allied with a chord relationship which eliminated complication of any kind. The whole trend of fifteenth century and sixteenth century teaching was in the direction of smoothness, of gliding progressions from one chord to another. The strict contrapuntal law permitted the use of only two chords, the triad and chord of the sixth. To these might be added certain suspensions, a device known as the *nota cambita*, which momentarily relaxed the strict rule that a discord was not allowed unprepared, and the freedom of passing-notes, which last, indeed, educated the ears of the musicians to many chords with a very modern sound. The result of these suave gliding harmonies was a very beautiful freedom, to which the absence of a leading note—or as sixteenth-century musicians would have expressed themselves—the sub-semitone to the Final undoubtedly contributed. With this curiously simple material Pierluigi united his *Canones in càncrizà* ; * his time combinations ; augmentations and diminutions of the theme ; yet the flow and effortlessness of these great works made them instruments fit for the service of the Church. It is impossible to consider them apart from their object.

Some seventy out of the amazing total of ninety masses † are based on fragments of the ancient church melodies—antiphones, hymns, sequences, or responses. The *Gloria* and *Credo* invariably waited on the opening liturgical chant of the officiating priest, the choir taking them up respectively at *Et in terra* and *Patrem omnipotentem.* These were not the only bonds imposed

* Or literally, crab-like canons, *i.e.* proceeding backwards.
† These figures are taken from Dr. Peter Wagner's *Geschichte der Messen.*

by the ritual. In the *Gloria* the tenor or *cantus firmus* must rise a major sixth to express *Tu solus altissimus*, a sufficiently unusual freedom of the voice-part to mark the significance of the words. Throughout the mass the composer was bound by the convention imposed by the ritual: the *Kyrie* with its three sections, the *Gloria* with two, the *Credo* two, possibly three, parts, the Sanctus three, the Benedictus two, the Agnus three. Such was the structure; the form of the mass, however, might be one of three types: *cantus firmus* masses, *choral* masses, and *missae parodiae*, that is, masses constructed over motets, madrigals, infrequently masses. The first mass Pierluigi published was a *cantus firmus* mass, *Ecce sacerdos magnus*, disqualified later, in conformity with the will of the Council of Trent, to rid the *Ordinarium* of interpolated text, or tropes. Another was the already mentioned hexachord mass which exhibits Pierluigi's invention at its highest, owing nothing—as it does—to the beauty of its theme, or even association.

GENERAL INDEX